DEPARTMENT OF HEALTH AND SOCIAL SECURITY
HOME OFFICE
WELSH OFFICE
LORD CHANCELLOR'S DEPARTMENT

# Review of the
# Mental Health Act 1959

*Presented to Parliament by the Secretary of State for Social Services, the Secretary of State for the Home Department, the Secretary of State for Wales and the Lord Chancellor*
*by Command of Her Majesty*
*September 1978*

*LONDON*
HER MAJESTY'S STATIONERY OFFICE
£2.00 net

Cmnd 7320

ISBN 0 10 173200 7

# CONTENTS

# INTRODUCTION

i. The Mental Health Act 1959 was based on the Report of the Royal Commission on the Law Relating to Mental Illness and Mental Deficiency* (the Percy Report). One of the basic premises of the Report was that people suffering from mental disorder should, as far as possible, be treated in the same way as those suffering from physical illnesses and that compulsion and custody should be used as little as possible. A range of safeguards was proposed for those patients who had to be the subject of compulsory powers and the Commission suggested that decisions on compulsory admission to hospital or guardianship should be a medical instead of a judicial matter. These proposals were embodied in the 1959 Act. The Act also contained a number of general provisions for the mentally ill and handicapped, but over the course of the past 18 years many of these have been removed from the Act and incorporated in other legislation. For example, Parts II and III have largely been replaced by other Acts, such as the Health Services and Public Health Act 1968 (the relevant provisions of which have been replaced in the National Health Service Act 1977), the Education (Handicapped Children) Act 1970 and the Nursing Homes Act 1975.

ii. In January 1975 the Government announced its intention to review the 1959 Mental Health Act in the light of the many changes which had taken place in treatment and care, in the patterns of services for the mentally ill and the mentally handicapped and in public attitudes.

iii. An Interdepartmental Committee of officials was set up to undertake the review—consisting of representatives of the Department of Health and Social Security, Welsh Office, Home Office and Lord Chancellor's Department. The Scottish Home and Health Department and the Department of Health and Social Services in Northern Ireland also sent observers, although their mental health legislation is separate from that for England and Wales and was not included in the review. The Committee had before it suggestions for amendment which had been made by the Royal College of Psychiatrists, the National Association for Mental Health (MIND), the Butler Committee** and other interested individuals and bodies.

iv. The Interdepartmental Committee started from the general premise that on the whole the Act had worked well but that there was clearly room for improvement in various respects and that some amendment would be of benefit to all concerned. The Committee's initial suggestions were set out in a Consultative Document,*** published in August 1976. Comments were invited from all interested bodies and individuals.

v. A one-day conference followed publication of the Consultative Document. This was well attended and provided a good opportunity for an exchange of views on the Document's contents. The response to the Document was also encouraging—comments being received from some 300 organisations and individuals. These were a very useful indicator of areas of consensus as well as of potential subjects of controversy. Following

---

\* Cmnd 169. HMSO (1957)

\*\* Cmnd 6244. *'Report of the Committee on Mentally Abnormal Offenders'*. HMSO (1975)

\*\*\* *'A Review of the Mental Health Act 1959'*. HMSO (1976). Hereafter referred to as 'the Consultive Document'

the publication of the Consultative Document two more major contributions to the debate came in the form of the second volume of MIND's 'A Human Condition' on offender patients and the British Association of Social Workers' document 'Mental Health Crisis Services—A New Philosophy'.

vi.   The Interdepartmental Committee studied all these comments before making recommendations to Ministers, and it is on the basis of this consultative exercise that this White Paper sets out the Government's proposals for change. The general philosophy behind the proposals is based on the need to strengthen the rights and safeguard the liberties of the mentally disordered whilst retaining a proper regard for the rights and safety of the general public and of staff.

vii.   The Government intends to translate most of the proposals in this White Paper into an amending Bill to be put before the House as soon as Parliamentary time can be found. However, in one or two cases the proposals are set out in a more tentative form because they were either not put forward in the Consultative Document or were not fully developed at that time. The most important topic which falls into this category is what compulsory powers, if any, are needed outside hospitals; this is discussed in Chapter 4 and comments are invited.

viii.   If the Wales Act 1978 receives the necessary majority in the referendum and is brought into effect it will devolve to a Welsh Assembly responsibility for providing health services and for making regulations under the 1959 Act. It will be for the Welsh Assembly to consider whether any changes in the services or in the regulations applying to Wales are needed. The proposals for change in the legislation outlined in this Paper will of course apply to Wales as well as to England.

ix.   Part VIII of the Act, which concerns the management of the property and affairs of patients, is not covered in this Paper. The Lord Chancellor will be considering separately whether any changes are desirable.

x.   Sections 127 and 128 of the Act relate to sexual offences; these are being considered by the Criminal Law Revision Committee, in the context of the review of the Sexual Offences Act 1956.

# CHAPTER 1

# THE SCOPE OF THE ACT AND THE DEFINITION
# OF MENTAL DISORDER

1.1 The scope of the Mental Health Act, as amended by subsequent legislation, is now largely limited to compulsory powers of admission to and detention in hospital, and to safeguards for patients subject to such powers. It is on these issues that this White Paper concentrates. Statutory powers for the provision of services for mentally ill and mentally handicapped people are contained in other legislation, and the underlying philosophy for the provision of such services has been outlined in other White Papers.* This Chapter considers whether changes are needed in the definition of mental disorder for the purpose of compulsory powers; but it also takes the opportunity to consider the position of informal (voluntary) patients, and whether any legislative change is required in respect of them.

## INFORMAL PATIENTS

1.2 Today, almost all mentally ill and mentally handicapped patients, whether in mental illness or mental handicap hospitals or in general hospital psychiatric units, are voluntary patients who are not detained under any of the powers of the Mental Health Act. They are referred to as 'informal' patients to distinguish them from patients detained under formal powers. That almost 90% of those admitted to mental illness and mental handicap hospitals and units and 95% of those resident there at any one time are informal patients is something of which the psychiatric services can be proud. It is testimony to the increasing confidence of the public in the services provided and to the increasing willingness on the part of patients and relatives alike to recognise the need for, and to accept, treatment.

1.3 In nearly all respects the position of informal psychiatric patients is the same as that of non-psychiatric patients but there are some differences. For example, section 134 of the Act extends to informal patients the power to withhold patients' mail; and section 90 authorises the Home Secretary in certain circumstances to remove from this country people who do not have the right of abode here and who are receiving treatment for mental illness as hospital in-patients. Section 141, which relates to legal actions undertaken by patients, is not entirely clear, but there is little doubt that it makes it difficult for an informal, as well as a compulsorily detained, patient to initiate a legal action against staff. An informal psychiatric patient who wishes to leave hospital may also, under section 30 of the Mental Health Act, be prevented from doing so for up to 3 days, pending an application for his compulsory detention under the Act, if the doctor in charge of his treatment believes this is necessary. This applies, however, to a patient in any hospital who becomes mentally disordered and cannot be said to differentiate informal psychiatric patients from others.

---

* Cmnd 4683. '*Better Services for the Mentally Handicapped*'. HMSO (1971).
  Cmnd 6233. '*Better Services for the Mentally Ill*'. HMSO (1975).

1

1.4    As explained in paragraphs 8.28, 8.8 and 7.10, below, the Government proposes to amend sections 90, 134 and 141 (respectively) so that they no longer apply to informal patients. If Parliament approves these changes the effect will be to remove all remaining legislative distinctions between informal patients in mental illness and mental handicap hospitals and units, and patients who are in hospital for some physical illness.* Such changes would be a significant step towards removing any stigma associated with admission to a mental illness or mental handicap hospital: and they would also help to remove the doubts which exist about the statutory position of informal patients.

1.5    It may be helpful to set out the position of informal patients as the Government sees it. An informal patient enters hospital on his doctor's advice to receive the care and treatment he is advised is necessary or desirable and he will normally stay in hospital until discharged by the consultant. These are voluntary acts on his part. He can insist on leaving hospital if he wishes and can decline to accept a particular form or course of treatment. If he does so the consultant may, of course, refuse to continue to accept responsibility for treating him but that does not affect the patient's right to insist on leaving or to refuse treatment.

1.6    There is nothing in the Act which authorises or implies that an informal patient may be compelled without his consent to enter hospital or to receive treatment. Nor does the Act contain any provision which authorises staff to lock an informal patient in a side room or detain him in a locked ward. In all these matters, the powers and responsibilities of doctors, nurses and other staff in relation to an informal patient are the same as those of staff to a patient in a non-psychiatric hospital. However, since staff, under common law, have a duty to offer treatment to patients and to take steps to supervise or control them in a way which will prevent them coming to harm the matter is not a simple one.

1.7    When a patient suffering from mental disorder is being admitted to hospital it will usually be clear whether or not he consents to such admission, but the issue may not always be clear-cut. It may to some extent depend on how far the patient understands that he is being admitted to hospital. In a patient who has the mental capacity to understand, at least in essence, what is taking place an absence on his part of objection to admission can be taken as implying consent. An initial refusal need not, of course, be taken as final. Initial reluctance may well be overcome with further explanation and reassurance. Or the patient may simply change his mind; confused old people are particularly likely to do so. But if, after full explanation and reasonable persuasion, the patient is unwilling to be admitted to hospital of his own free will and consent, no matter how unreasonable this may seem, the only choices so far as admission to hospital are concerned are either to admit him to hospital under compulsory powers or not to admit him. If he is not to be admitted to hospital attempts should of course be made to persuade him to receive treatment on an out-patient basis or from his family doctor.

* The Government has accepted in principle the recommendation of the 1973/4 Speaker's Conference that patients in mental hospitals should be treated similarly to those in general hospitals for electoral registration purposes.

1.8   Where the patient does not have the mental capacity to know what is taking place an absence of objection on his part cannot in law be taken either as implying or withholding consent to admission. In practice of course, in such cases, admission to hospital is unlikely to be challenged so long as it is evident to all concerned that the staff have acted in the best interests of their patient. It may however be prudent to record reasons for admission. Where there is any doubt or likelihood of dispute, for example from relatives, as to whether a proposed admission is in the patient's best interests the appointment of a guardian under the Mental Health Act, who can give or withhold consent on the patient's behalf, should be considered. Failing that, the patient should not be admitted to hospital except under compulsory powers.

1.9   It is emphasised above that the powers, duties and responsibilities of doctors, nurses and other staff in relation to an informal patient who has been admitted to hospital are the same as those of staff in relation to a patient in a non-psychiatric hospital. But, as explained above, all staff, whether in psychiatric or general hospitals, have a duty under common law to prevent patients coming to harm; for example they have a duty to prevent a confused patient from wandering—whether the confusion is due to drugs or defect or deterioration of the brain—if, by doing so, the patient would be putting himself or others at risk. It may sometimes be difficult, however, for staff to know how far they should go in restraining an informal patient who asks to leave hospital but whom the staff think it would be unwise to allow to do so. Indeed it may be difficult—especially in the case of an elderly confused person—to tell whether an expression of desire to leave hospital is a passing whim rather a real wish. Clearly in such cases staff should always, where the patient has sufficient understanding, try to persuade him to remain. The persuasion should not go to excessive lengths, however. If the patient cannot be persuaded to remain of his own free will he must either be allowed to leave the hospital or, if the appropriate criteria are met, be detained under the compulsory powers provided by the Act.

1.10   Where an informal patient is not capable of understanding where he is or the fact that he is being prevented from leaving, an absence of protest cannot, of course, be taken as implying consent to detention; but action to prevent such a patient from wandering and possibly doing himself harm is unlikely to be challenged. This situation may arise particularly with elderly severely mentally infirm people, with the severely mentally handicapped, and a few mentally ill patients.

1.11   In an emergency staff may have to put an informal patient for a short period in a locked room or ward or impose some form of treatment—eg a sedative—for the safety of all concerned. In such cases they would have a justification in law if such action is immediately necessary to save life, or prevent violence or serious deterioration in the patient's condition. Staff may also, under section 3(1) of the Criminal Law Act 1967, use such force as is reasonable in the circumstances prevailing at the time to prevent a violent or dangerous act which would amount to a crime.

In situations other than these, the usual course, where it is considered necessary to seclude a patient or to impose treatment, must be to seek proper authority under an appropriate section of the Mental Health Act. This also applies where it can be foreseen that emergencies are likely to recur. Where the patient does not have the capacity to consent to treatment, consideration should be given to appointing a guardian with powers to consent or refuse treatment on his behalf.

1.12 Staff are naturally anxious to avoid invoking compulsory powers as far as possible, and often feel that it is in the patient's long term interest that he should not be compulsorily admitted or detained. However well-intentioned this may be, it sometimes leads staff to controlling and treating patients in a way which goes beyond legal authority and exposes staff to the risk of legal action. It is appreciated that a stricter regard to the rights of informal patients in this respect might lead to more patients being made the subject of compulsory powers than is now the case, but it should be noted that the taking of compulsory powers also brings with it safeguards (application to a Mental Health Review Tribunal etc.) not available to informal patients.

1.13 It will never, though, be possible to legislate for every eventuality. Nor would the invoking of compulsory powers provide staff with the answer to every problem that might arise. There will be instances in which it might be better for staff to rely upon the powers in section 3(1) of the Criminal Law Act and the common law doctrine referred to above, together with the implied agreement by patients who have voluntarily entered hospital that they will comply with general standards of reasonable behaviour and the rules of the hospital and be prepared to receive some form of treatment. It would of course also help if reasons for actions taken are recorded and kept with the patient's case notes in case any query is later raised.

1.14 It is recognized that with the threat of compulsory powers in the background some informal patients will, rightly or wrongly, feel themselves to be under a degree of coercion. Others, whilst not detained under the Mental Health Act may, because of their mental state, be unable to assert a wish to leave the hospital or to refuse consent to a particular form of treatment. There have also been occasions when it has not been made clear to patients that they have ceased to be subject to compulsory powers and that as informal patients they are free to leave hospital if they wish. All this does not mean that informal status needs revision but it may indicate a need for additional safeguards. The Government therefore proposes the following measures—

    i. On admission of an informal patient to hospital he should be given a written statement of his rights including his right to leave hospital if he wishes and his right to refuse any particular form of treatment. The statement should however point out that, in agreeing to enter hospital, he is assumed to be willing to receive some treatment and that if he wishes to leave hospital against medical advice he should tell his doctor or the nursing staff beforehand and should wait until day-time before leaving.

ii. Where a patient's status is changed from that of an informal patient to that of a detained patient (or vice versa) the patient should be informed in writing within 24 hours of the change in status and of the conditions and rights appropriate to his new status. Any subsequent changes, eg from detention under section 29 or 30 to that under section 25 or 26 or when powers lapse or are not renewed, should be notified in the same way.

iii. Where treatment of an irreversible nature, or treatment which is not fully established or which may carry disproportionate risks is proposed to be carried out on an informal patient, the doctor should be required to explain what is involved in terms which the patient can understand and to obtain the patient's express agreement and to seek a second opinion before undertaking treatment. Fuller definition of the treatments concerned and discussion of the arrangements for providing a second opinion are contained in Chapter 6 below.

The possible introduction of a scheme of patients' advisers to help informal patients, particularly long stay patients, to understand and exercise their rights, is also discussed in Chapter 6 (particularly paragraph 6.35).

## THE DEFINITION OF MENTAL DISORDER

1.15 Mental disorder is defined in section 4 of the Mental Health Act as: 'mental illness, arrested or incomplete development of mind, psychopathic disorder and any other disorder or disability of mind'. The section sets out four sub-categories of mental disorder:

    i. mental illness;

    ii. subnormality;

    iii. severe subnormality;

    iv. psychopathic disorder.

The section includes definitions of subnormality, severe subnormality and psychopathic disorder but does not attempt a definition of mental illness.

1.16 The Consultative Document* discussed the present definition of mental disorder and its sub-categories and sought comments on three alternative methods of definition and on a suggestion from MIND** that compulsory admission and detention should be based on behavioural criteria alone. The alternatives were—

    i. a general definition of mental disorder, with no attempt to break this down into sub-categories;

    ii. precise definitions of sub-categories of mental disorder and exclusion of the open-ended term 'any other disorder or disability of mind';

    iii. retention of a general definition of mental disorder with improvements in the definition of the sub-categories.

---

\* Paras 1.6 to 1.26.

\*\* 'A Human Condition: The Mental Health Act from 1959 to 1975'. MIND publication (1975). Vol I, pp. 33–35.

1.17 Comments on the Document showed little support for MIND's suggestion that admission should be based on behavioural criteria alone or for alternative ii. which was generally felt to be too restrictive and to be likely to lead to problems in practice. Alternatives i. and iii. received an almost equal measure of support. Alternative i. would allow greater width of interpretation, obviate the need for further amendment in the light of future developments in psychiatry, simplify this part of the Act, and help to prevent the attachment to patients of diagnostic labels (eg 'psychopathic' or 'subnormal'), labels which tend to remain throughout life. However, it would widen the scope of compulsory powers by bringing within the powers of compulsory detention beyond 28 days patients in the category 'any other disorder or disability of mind'. (These powers apply now only to patients in the 4 sub-categories referred to in para 1.15). No substantial argument for such a widening of powers has been advanced. However undesirable labelling may be, it is unlikely to be avoided entirely. Furthermore, the present method of specifying sub-categories does have the advantage of allowing those suffering from different disorders to be dealt with in different ways and adds a valuable flexibility in the use of compulsory powers. Thus, although a general definition would simplify this part of the Act, this is not thought to outweigh the attendant disadvantages. It is therefore proposed that the present definition of mental disorder by reference to sub-categories should continue but that the definitions of subnormality, severe subnormality and psychopathic disorder should be revised. There have been a few suggestions as to how mental illness might be defined, but comments have underlined the difficulties of producing a definition which would be likely to stand the test of time. Nor has there been much evidence that the present lack of definition of mental illness leads to any particular problems; the Government therefore proposes to leave it undefined.

**Should Mental Handicap be Included Within the Scope of the Act?**

1.18 One criticism of the Mental Health Act is that it brings mental illness and mental handicap under the same general legislative provisions. Mental illness and mental handicap are still often confused with one another. The Consultative Document* in discussing whether mental handicap should be removed from the scope of the Act recognised that its inclusion may give the impression of equating it with other forms of mental incapacity. However, it also recognised that mentally handicapped people were more usually detained in hospital under compulsory powers not because of intellectual retardation or diminished social competence as such but because their behaviour appeared to present a threat either to themselves or to others. Similarly it is the behaviour of some mentally ill people which warrants their detention rather than the mental illness itself.

1.19 This part of the Document aroused much comment and interest. Very few suggested that no legislative provisions were required for the

* Appendix III.

mentally handicapped. Most felt that compulsion would continue to be needed in a small number of cases to safeguard both the public and mentally handicapped people themselves. Of the majority who thought legislative provision was required, most felt this should be within the Mental Health Act although a substantial number favoured separate legislation. There seems to be a fairly general recognition that, although most of the mentally handicapped can and should receive the care and training they need on a voluntary basis, there is a need to retain some compulsory powers. Much of the opposition to retaining mental handicap within the scope of the Mental Health Act is apparently based on the misinterpretation that this implies that it is appropriate to detain people in hospital simply because they are mentally handicapped. The Government's view is that mental handicap needs to be retained within the scope of the Act but that it would also be helpful to include a declaratory provision in the Act to the effect that the mere presence of mental handicap—or indeed any other form of mental disorder—does not by itself justify the use of compulsory powers. Such powers should only be invoked where the other criteria for compulsory admission or detention are also met. These criteria are discussed in Chapters 2 and 3 below.

1.20   The Government has considered whether there should be a separate Act for the mentally handicapped. Whilst this would have the advantage of avoiding confusion, there would seem little point in having separate Acts of Parliament for mental illness and for mental handicap unless their content is to differ significantly. Most of the areas discussed in this White Paper concern both the mentally ill and the mentally handicapped, and it is proposed to maintain the powers and safeguards within the same Act but to ensure that distinctions are made where appropriate.

1.21   The terms 'subnormality' and 'severe subnormality' cause offence and distress and it is proposed that they should be replaced by 'mental handicap' and 'severe mental handicap'. It is also proposed to amend the definitions of these two sub-categories. The present definition of subnormality refers only to level of intelligence, but it is now felt that the behavioural aspects of mental handicap must be adequately recognised; it is thus proposed to refer to a state of arrested or incomplete development of mind which includes significant impairment of intelligence and social functioning. Severe mental handicap should be acknowledged to be a more extreme form of the same disability rather than a separate condition. Here, too, the effect on social behaviour and functioning must be stressed since this is the basis on which handicap is included in the Act. The definition of severe mental handicap would thus refer to a state of arrested or incomplete development of mind which includes severe impairment of intelligence and social functioning.

1.22   The present definition of subnormality refers to susceptibility to medical treatment or other special care or training. While the prospect of such benefit is an important consideration in determining the use of compulsory powers it need not be relevant in every case where powers under the Act are invoked. For example, it may be desirable to seek powers of

_____
* Paras 1.20 to 1.26.

control over a severely mentally handicapped person in order to protect him from exploitation even when there is little likelihood of benefit from treatment or other special care or training. It seems more appropriate to consider this question in relation to the criteria for compulsory hospital admission rather than in relation to the definition of mental handicap as such. These criteria are discussed in paragraphs 2.38 to 2.42, below.

1.23 At present, the Act refers to treatment as 'medical treatment', which is defined to include care and training being given 'under medical supervision'. Wide though this definition is, it may be too restrictive in relation to modern treatment programmes for the mentally handicapped; and a new definition of treatment which makes it clear that it includes care, training, the use of habilitative techniques and medical, nursing and other professional help would be more in line with today's perception of the needs of the mentally handicapped whilst still covering the treatment needs of other groups of the mentally disordered.

**Psychopathic Disorder**
1.24 There is doubt about whether psychopathic disorder should be included within the scope of the Act at all since it is questionable whether the Health Service can at present offer effective treatment to the generality of people suffering from this disorder. However, the Consultative Document,* whilst recognising this, felt that the possibility of some future advance in treatment should not be ruled out and that it would not be right to deny all possibility of compulsory hospital treatment to psychopaths as an alternative to prison. Whilst widely divergent views on this issue were expressed, the majority favoured retaining within the Mental Health Act some powers in relation to psychopaths. MIND are critical of retaining powers in relation to a form of mental disorder which is neither clearly definable nor considered treatable, but they do not suggest that psychopathic disorder should be removed from the Act altogether. They have suggested that psychopaths should only be detainable under hospital orders made by courts under Part V of the Act. The Government's view is that powers should be retained to enable the compulsory admission to hospital of persons suffering from psychopathic disorder irrespective of whether they have committed a criminal offence.

1.25 The Butler Committee wished to see the term psychopathic disorder replaced by 'personality disorder'; they also recommended** that a court order for detention in hospital should not be made "in the case of an offender suffering from psychopathic disorder with dangerous anti-social tendencies unless the court is satisfied:
(a) That a previous mental or organic illness, or an identifiable psychological or physical defect, relevant to the disorder is known or suspected; and
(b) there is an expectation of therapeutic benefit from hospital admission."

---

* Paras. 1.20 to 1.26
** Cmnd 6244. Paras 5.24 to 5.26 and 5.40

1.26 Comments on the Consultative Document gave little backing to the proposal that the term 'personality disorder' be adopted. However, there was considerable support for the recommendation on the conditions under which a court may make a hospital order and in particular on the need for an expectation of therapeutic benefit from admission. Despite this, the Government has decided not to adopt the formula suggested by the Butler Committee since the wording, particularly in (a), is complex and its practical effect in terms of the number of psychopaths admitted to hospital from court is uncertain. Some believe it would make no difference whilst others feel it would markedly reduce the numbers. However, the Government accepts that the Act should establish a clear requirement that psychopaths should only be detained under compulsory powers where there is a good prospect of benefit from treatment. The present definition of psychopathic disorder includes the wording 'and requires or is susceptible to medical treatment'. The Government proposes that this should be omitted from the definition in section 4 of the Act, since it does not seem appropriate as part of a definition, but that a 'prospect of benefit from treatment' requirement should instead be incorporated into the criteria for compulsory admission and renewal of detention. This is discussed in paragraphs 2.38 to 2.45, below.

1.27 MIND have suggested that it should be permissible for a court to make hospital orders under section 60 in relation to psychopathic offenders only in respect of those who have expressed a positive preference for admission to hospital rather than prison. Whilst there is little point in sending a psychopath to hospital if he is clearly not prepared to co-operate with treatment the Government does not feel it would be appropriate for the court's decision on the disposal of a psychopathic offender to be a matter for the offender to decide, and in any case there would be practical difficulties. For example, courts could not take measures in advance of a defendant's trial to find out if a hospital place was available, and this might lead to offenders having to be remanded for some time whilst a suitable place was found.

**Drug and Alcohol Abuse and Sexual Deviancy**

1.28 The Consultative Document* referred to the fact that powers of compulsory admission or detention were sometimes usefully employed in relation to alcoholics or drug addicts. The power compulsorily to admit for observation (under section 25) a person suffering from 'any other disorder or disability of the mind' seems often to be invoked to provide temporary protection for an alcoholic or addict who is a danger to himself and to determine whether or not there is an underlying mental disorder.

1.29 Very little comment was received on this point. However, it was suggested that it should be made clear that compulsory powers should not be invoked because of alcohol or drug dependence in themselves but only where the dependency gave rise to a mental disorder which would in its own right warrant the use of compulsion. Government advisory bodies have also pointed out that it is incompatible with current thinking on the nature

---

* Para 1.13.

of drug dependence and drinking problems to regard them as mental disorders. These conditions are increasingly seen as social and behavioural problems, manifested in varying degrees of habit and dependency. However, it is recognised that alcohol or drug dependency can be associated with certain forms of mental disorder.

1.30 The Government proposes that the Act should include a specific provision excluding alcohol and drug dependency in themselves from its terms. This would not, however, rule out the possibility of a person being detained on the grounds of a mental disorder arising from, or suspected to arise from, alcohol or drug dependence or from the withdrawal of alcohol or a drug—and this would be made clear either in legislation or subsequent guidance to health authorities.

1.31 Since it is recommended below (paragraph 2.12) that section 25 should be made a treatment as well as an assessment order, it may be advisable also to make it clear that the Act does not permit treatment to be imposed on a person suffering from alcohol or drug dependence except where the patient is being detained on the grounds of mental disorder arising from, or suspected to arise from, alcohol or drug dependence or from the withdrawal of alcohol or a drug. Again, this might either be made clear in the Act itself or in subsequent guidance to health authorities.

1.32. The Government thinks the Act should make it clear that sexual deviancy of itself is not a mental disorder and does not provide sufficient grounds for compulsory detention in hospital. It therefore proposes the inclusion of a new provision excluding sexual deviancy as well as drug or alcohol dependence from the scope of the Act. Where a mentally disordered person commits a sexual offence it will of course remain open to the court to consider making a hospital order under section 60 instead of a penal disposal.

SUMMARY OF PROPOSALS:   CHAPTER 1

*Informal patients*

   i.   All informal patients, on admission to hospital, should be given a written statement of their rights (para 1.14)

   ii.   If a patient's status is changed from informal to detained (or vice versa) he should be informed in writing within 24 hours of the change in status and of the conditions and rights attached to the new status (para 1.14)

   iii.   Where it is proposed to give an informal patient a treatment which is either irreversible, not fully established or which carries disproportionate risks, the doctor should be required to seek the express consent of the patient and a second opinion before the treatment is carried out (para 1.14)

*Scope of Act and definitions*

   iv.   Mental disorder should continue to be defined as at present, ie with reference to sub-categories (paras 1.15 to 1.17)

v. Mental illness should remain undefined (para 1.17)

vi. Mental handicap should be retained within the scope of the Act (paras 1.18 to 1.20)

vii. The terms 'subnormality' and 'severe subnormality' should be replaced by 'mental handicap' and 'severe mental handicap' (para 1.21)

viii. New definitions for mental handicap and severe mental handicap should be introduced (para 1.22)

ix. The definition of treatment should be amended to make it clear that treatment includes care, training, the use of habilitative techniques and medical, nursing or other professional help (para 1.23)

x. The term 'psychopathic disorder' should be retained and the definition of psychopathic disorder should remain as it is, except that the clause 'and requires or is susceptible to medical treatment' should be omitted from the definition; a requirement that there is a likelihood of benefit from treatment should be incorporated into the criteria for compulsory admission and renewal of detention for persons suffering from psychopathic disorder (paras 1.24 to 1.26)

xi. Alcohol and drug dependence in themselves should not be regarded as mental disorders and are to be excluded from the scope of the Act (para 1.30)

xii. Sexual deviancy of itself is not a mental disorder and should be excluded from the terms of the Act (para 1.32).

## CHAPTER 2

# COMPULSORY ADMISSION TO AND DETENTION IN HOSPITAL

2.1   The Mental Health Act provides short-term and longer term powers for compulsory admission to and detention in hospital. At 31 December 1976, there were about 1,100 people in hospital detained under short term powers and 5,300 under longer term powers (section 26 and 60).

### THE SHORT TERM POWERS

2.2   The short term powers are:
   i. emergency admission for observation under section 29;
   ii. admission for observation and assessment under section 25;
   iii. removal to a place of safety under section 135;
   iv. power of constable to remove a person from a public place under section 136;
   v. short term detention of an informal patient already in hospital under section 30.

### Emergency admission for observation (Section 29).

2.3   Section 29 provides, in a case of urgent necessity, for the compulsory admission to hospital of a patient for observation. 12,000 people were admitted in this way in 1976. An application can be made by any relative (as defined by the Act) or by a Mental Welfare Officer, on the basis of a recommendation by any doctor. The section authorises detention for up to 72 hours only, unless the second medical recommendation which is required for the use of section 25 is obtained within that period. The intention of the 1959 Act was that compulsory admission for observation should normally be under section 25 and that section 29 should be used only in emergencies when there was not enough time to obtain the second medical recommendation. Section 29 has however been invoked more frequently than originally envisaged, and it has become the most widely used form of compulsory admission. There is also wide regional variation in its use. The Government hopes that the increasing development of the 24-hour crisis intervention services envisaged in the White Paper 'Better Services for the Mentally Ill'* will in time reduce the need for such admissions, by enabling some emergencies to be contained without the need for compulsory admission to hospital or alternatively for two medical assessments to be provided. However, given the present constraints on manpower and resources, it is accepted that there is a continuing need for a statutory emergency procedure. While there is a good deal of support in comments on the Consultative-Document for developing 24-hour crisis intervention services and for the view that these would reduce the use of section 29, it was also argued

* Cmnd 6233. Para 3.12.

that, however fully developed, crisis intervention services could never adequately replace section 29 powers, particularly in rural areas. Comments included the point that section 29 allows for a short assessment or 'cooling off' period which can often lead to discharge within 72 hours or to the person staying in hospital as an informal patient.

2.4 The extent of regional variation in the use of section 29 powers attracted a good deal of comment. Community Health Councils were particularly critical that the powers are sometimes used to suit administrative expediency. Cases were cited where hospitals had made a rule that no informal admission should be accepted after 5 pm with the result that any admission after this time had to be a compulsory admission, usually under section 29. Any such rule still in being should clearly be discontinued, and hospital managers should ensure that adequate arrangements exist for the emergency admission of both voluntary and compulsory patients.

2.5 The value of a short period for 'cooling off' or for assessment is accepted, and it is proposed to amend section 29 to provide for its use for these purposes. A fuller statement of the reasons why urgent admission is necessary and a statement by the Mental Welfare Officer and the medical signatory of why it was not possible to obtain a second medical recommendation will however be required. Scrutiny of these statements by the hospital managers would provide a check that adequate explanation for compulsory detention had been given and that emergency powers had not been used for administrative convenience.

2.6 At present, the Act requires an applicant for emergency admission to have seen the patient within three days of making the application; completion of the application gives authority for the patient's conveyance to hospital within three days from the date of the medical examination or the making of the application, whichever is the earlier. These lengths of time seem hardly consonant with a need for emergency admission. It is therefore proposed—

    i. that the maximum period within which the applicant must personally have seen the patient should be reduced from three days to 24 hours;

    ii. that an admission should take place within 24 hours of the medical examination or application (whichever is the earlier) instead of three days.

These changes should help to prevent section 29 being used for cases other than those of real emergency.

2.7 Paragraph 3.16 below proposes that only the nearest relative (or a Mental Welfare Officer) should be able to apply for admission and not 'any relative' as is allowed under section 29 at present.

2.8 The present wording of section 29 ties the use of its powers to hospitals and this is proving inflexible in the development of crisis intervention services. It has therefore been suggested that section 29 should allow a person's removal to a 'place of assessment' and that this should be defined to include any local authority social services or health authority accommodation, as well as a hospital. If compulsory powers in the community are to be introduced (as discussed in Chapter 4 below) this would seem an essential requirement, as would power to convert an emergency order into a short term community order.

## Compulsory admission for observation and assessment (Section 25)

2.9   Section 25 provides for compulsory admission to hospital for observation, and for detention for this purpose for up to 28 days. It was intended to enable the patient's condition to be assessed. The mental disorder must be such as to warrant detention in hospital for observation in the interests of the patient's own health or safety or with a view to the protection of other people. Use of the section has gradually declined from 11,912 admissions in 1966 to 6,868 in 1976. The Consultative Document* discussed MIND's proposal that the power should be removed but suggested that it was useful and should be retained. It also discussed doubts about the extent to which the section authorised treatment to be imposed without consent and suggested that the Act might be clarified to limit compulsory treatment to that necessary to prevent violence or to save life.

### Section 25 as a treatment order?

2.10   At present section 25 provides for the detention of a patient for 'observation with or without other medical treatment' but does not explicitly allow treatment to be imposed without consent. The view of DHSS legal advisers is that section 25 provides authority for treatment of a patient without his consent but that such treatment cannot exceed what is reasonably required by way of observation, ie for the purpose of diagnosis and the determination of what future care may be appropriate or is immediately necessary in the interests of the patient's own health or safety or for the protection of others. The comments received indicated that the powers are often interpreted more widely; indeed a number of comments have supported the retention of section 25 on the grounds that it provides a short period of detention in which effective treatment can be given. The Royal College of Psychiatrists' view is that the essential purpose of all compulsory admission and detention must be treatment and that section 25 is commonly used for treatment as well as observation; in most cases discharge or change to informal status occurs within the 28-day period. Others have commented that the distinction between observation and treatment is by no means clear. The Royal College has recommended that section 25 should remain the normal basis for compulsory admission and that it should be explicitly established in law as a short term observation and treatment order.

2.11   This would broaden the range of mental disorders for which a person can be compulsorily detained for treatment since section 25 extends to patients suffering from any disorder or disabilty of mind rather than being limited to the specific categories of disorder referred to in section 4 of the Act. A further point of consideration is that there are fewer safeguards for patients under section 25 than under section 26. MIND for example argue that it is wrong to detain for up to 28 days without there being a right of appeal.

---

* Paras 2.11 to 2.14.

2.12  If, as professional opinion suggests, developments in psychiatric practice now mean that compulsory detention in hospital often need not last longer than 28 days and that most patients either become informal patients or are discharged within that period, this should clearly be recognised in legislation. Moreover, the distinction between observation and treatment does not seem sufficiently clear to warrant a separate observation order. It is therefore proposed that section 25 should explicitly provide for short term assessment and treatment. The term 'assessment' seems more appropriate than 'observation'. The Act should however—

    i.  make clear the mental disorders in respect of which a patient can be subject to compulsory detention under a section 25 order; and

    ii.  provide stronger safeguards for patients detained under the section.

The following paragraphs set out the Government's proposals for meeting these points.

## The scope of section 25

2.13  At present one of the criteria for compulsory detention for treatment under longer term compulsory powers (ie under sections 26 or 60) is that the patient must be suffering from one of four specified categories of mental disorder (see paragraph 1.15, above) whereas under section 25 he can also be suffering from 'any other disorder or disability of mind'. Section 25 has in practice been used to provide a short term period of compulsory detention and treatment for people in an abnormal state of mind, for example following a drug overdose or a bereavement. This flexibility is generally thought to serve a useful and humane purpose, and it is proposed to leave the scope of section 25 unchanged, but as recorded in paragraphs 1.30 and 1.32, above, the Government proposes that sexual deviancy or drug or alcohol dependence should not of themselves be regarded as mental disorder.

## Safeguards in relation to section 25

2.14  The Consultative Document* recommended that section 29 applications should give fuller information about the reasons why compulsory admission and detention were essential and why less formal arrangements were not appropriate or practicable. To back this up it was suggested that the forms should be closely scrutinised. Comments generally supported this view and it follows that, if section 25 is to become a treatment as well as an assessment order, the case for tighter control is even stronger. It is proposed that the statement of reasons for detention should indicate from which category of mental disorder the patient is suffering or is suspected to be suffering and, where the recommendation is made on the ground of 'any disorder or disability of mind', the particular form of mental disorder suspected.

2.15  The safeguards for patients detained under section 26 are stronger than those for patients under section 25. For example, the Mental Welfare Officer is required to consult the nearest relative where an application is being made for detention under section 26 except where this is not practic-

---

* Para 2.10.

able or would cause unreasonable delay. If the nearest relative objects to the application being made, the Mental Welfare Officer cannot proceed. However, on the application of the Mental Welfare Officer or any relative of the patient or any other person with whom the patient is living, a County Court can make an order appointing another person to act as the nearest relative in certain circumstances, for instance where it is established that the nearest relative has unreasonably objected to an application for compulsory admission. In view of the delay which can be involved in this procedure, it is not thought practicable for the patient's nearest relative to have a similar right to veto a section 25 application but it is proposed that the Mental Welfare Officer should be required to take all reasonable steps to inform the nearest relative that a section 25 application has been made and to tell him of his rights of discharge and appeal (see paragraph 3.15 below). It is considered that the nearest relative should have the same right to discharge a section 25 patient as he does a section 26 patient, but with the same provisos: that the relative should give at least 72 hours' notice of his intention of ordering discharge and that the discharge should be subject to the veto of the Responsible Medical Officer on the grounds either of need to protect others from serious harm or of the grave incapacity of the patient.

2.16 The 'managers' of mental illness and handicap hospitals (who are in most cases the relevant Area Health Authority) have powers under section 47 to discharge patients detained under the Act (other than patients subject to a restriction order—see para 5.10 below); in practice these powers seem to be little used. It would be helpful to establish formal procedures so that patients and their relatives have a clear understanding of their right to ask the managers to exercise their power of discharge and can be assured that such applications are considered speedily and fully. It is proposed that, where a patient asks the managers to review his case, they should be required to arrange for him to be interviewed on their behalf within 3 days and to give their decision within a further 7 days. This should also apply to patients under sections 26 and 60. It is proposed that a patient should have the right of one such appeal to the managers during the 28 day period of detention under section 25, and perhaps two per year for patients detained for longer periods.

2.17 The most effective safeguard against unwarranted detention is thought to be review by a Mental Health Review Tribunal, but it would rarely be practicable to arrange a full Tribunal hearing in time for a decision to be reached within the 28 days' duration of the order. Some more limited review might be provided and it is intended to investigate this further before amending legislation is introduced.

2.18 As the Act stands at present, a patient cannot be detained under section 25 for more than 28 days. After that time, if he is to remain in hospital, he must either do so as an informal patient or be detained under section 26 of the Act. The Government believes this should continue to be the position. If a patient's condition requires his detention beyond 28 days it is important that the stronger safeguards of a section 26 order are available to him. There is some evidence that section 25 orders have been renewed on occasions; it is proposed to make it clear that this is improper.

**Power to Enter Premises and Remove to a 'Place of Safety' (Section 135)**

2.19 It may on rare occasions be necessary to enter private premises without the permission of the occupant in order to remove a person thought to be mentally disordered to a 'place of safety', so that his condition can be assessed and arrangements made for his care and treatment. Section 135 provides for three circumstances—

i. where a mentally disordered person is being ill-treated, neglected, or not kept under proper control;

ii. where he is unable to care for himself and living alone;

iii. where he is subject to detention under the Act and is absent from hospital without leave, and entry to the premises has been, or is likely to be, refused.

Under section 135 a magistrate may issue a warrant authorising a constable to enter premises, if necessary by force, for this purpose. In the case of i. and ii. above the magistrate must first have had evidence on oath from a Mental Welfare Officer, and both a Mental Welfare Officer and a doctor must accompany the constable when carrying out the warrant.

2.20 Only 13 people were admitted to hospital under section 135 in 1976. The very few comments received endorsed the view of the Consultative Document* that, although seldom invoked, it is a useful power which should be retained.

2.21 The Faculty of Community Medicine of the Royal College of Physicians, however, thought that the section should also provide for a situation where two mentally disordered people were living together and were unable to care for themselves. At present the power can only be exercised where a person unable to care for himself is living alone. Such an amendment would clearly be useful in the rare cases where a situation like this arises. It is therefore proposed that section 135 be retained and that the amendment be incorporated.

**Constable's Power to Remove a Person from a Public Place (Section 136)**

2.22 Section 136(1) empowers a police constable to remove a person from a public place to a 'place of safety' if he appears to be suffering from mental disorder and to be in immediate need of care and control and if the constable thinks it necessary to remove him in his own interests or for the protection of other people. Usually, this arises where a person's abnormal behaviour is causing nuisance or offence. Section 136(2) authorises such a person's detention in a place of safety for up to 72 hours so that he can be examined by a doctor and be interviewed by a Mental Welfare Officer and so that any necessary arrangements can be made for his treatment or care. The use of the power has, according to national statistics, been fairly constant over the last few years, there being some 1600 cases in 1976. However, the Butler Committee** drew attention to the need to interpret these statistics with care.

---

* Para 2.26.
** Cmnd 6244. Paras 9.4 to 9.6.

2.23    The Consultative Document* suggested that the section provides a useful power which should be retained but that its use should be more carefully monitored. A good deal of comment was received, mostly in favour of retention. MIND have suggested implementing the Royal Commission's recommendation that the police should only be able to compel a person to go to hospital if his behaviour would render him liable to arrest under normal police powers. Although there was some support for this proposal on the grounds that the very extensive powers of arrest of the police allow sufficient flexibility, many others thought such a condition too restrictive. The Government does not propose to limit the use of section 136 in this way.

*A Police Station as a 'Place of Safety'*

2.24 ˙  The major difficulty with section 136 appears to be in its implementation rather than its principle; and in particular whether, as the Consultative Document** suggested, a hospital should normally be the 'place of safety' and whether police stations should ever be used as such. A 'place of safety' as defined in the Act can be local authority social services accommodation, a hospital, a police station, a mental nursing home, a residential home for mentally disordered persons or 'any other suitable place' the occupier of which is willing temporarily to receive the person. Most comments agreed that police stations should not normally be used as places of safety for this purpose since they are not places where a sick person, possibly in a distressed condition, should have to remain for any appreciable time. However, there is also general agreement that there are circumstances in which detention in a police station is necessary and that this possibility should be retained as a last resort. A number of comments favoured adopting the Scottish Mental Health Act requirement that a police station should only be used if in an emergency there is no other suitable place available for receiving the patient.

2.25    The Government believes that the best course would be to retain the power in its present form and to leave the definition of a place of safety as it stands. It proposes however to issue guidance following legislation amending the Act to make it clear that a police station should only be used where a more appropriate place for assessment is not immediately available or where the person concerned is in transit to an appropriate place. It also intends to make it clear that the section 136 power expires once the person has been medically examined, has been interviewed by a Mental Welfare Officer and any necessary arrangements have been made for his treatment or care, or after 72 hours whichever is the earlier.

*A Hospital as a 'Place of Safety'*

2.26    Whilst a hospital will be recommended as the usual 'place of safety' the Government is aware of the operational difficulties which have been encountered. There is an understandable reluctance in some hospitals to undertake this role since staff feel that they are being asked to accept

---

* Paras 2.20 to 2.30.
** Para 2.27.

responsibility for the custody and care of someone who is possibly violent or a nuisance but whose need for hospital treatment has not been assessed. This perhaps arises from some misunderstanding about the purpose of section 136. There is clearly a widespread impression that the act of removing someone to hospital under section 136 is tantamount to their formal admission as a patient. In fact, the section only authorises a person's removal to a place of safety for the purpose of medical examination and interview by a Mental Welfare Officer and the making of any necessary arrangements for his treatment or care. Once these have taken place the power lapses. It may be out-patient or day-patient treatment that is required—or local authority social services—rather than admission to hospital. If the patient needs to be admitted to hospital and is not willing to enter as an informal patient then consideration must be given to whether his condition warrants detention under either section 25 or section 26. If he is not to be admitted as an in-patient he is of course free to leave, although any arrangements for other treatment and care should, where possible, be made before he does so.

2.27   The operational difficulties that have arisen are not the sort which can be overcome by legislative change, and it may be preferable to draw up general guidance or a code of practice allowing sufficient flexibility to enable local arrangements to be tailored to the facilities available. Health and local authorities and the police might be asked to agree on the particular places in their area to be designated as places of safety for section 136 purposes. These would normally be hospitals but local authority accommodation should also be considered where appropriate facilities are available.

2.28   The Consultative Document* suggested that fuller explanation should be given when section 136 powers were used and that this should be subject to monitoring. At present there is no statutory form, equivalent to those used for sections 25, 26 and 29, stating the reasons for the use by the police of section 136: at least one police force has already found such a form, developed independently for internal use, helpful in respect of their exercise of section 136 powers. The main value of a form to accompany the patient is to explain the circumstances in which he was found and why the police thought he was in urgent need of care and control. The Government believes that the best course would be for the DHSS to negotiate with the police and with the health and local authorities what information might be required and an appropriate form could then be recommended in guidance. The same monitoring arrangements could be used as with other compulsory admission procedures; there could, however, be no question of the monitoring leading to a challenge of the legality of police actions.

**Short Term Detention of a Patient Already in Hospital (Section 30)**

2.29   Section 30 provides for an application to be made for compulsory detention where a person who is mentally disordered is already an in-patient in any hospital and it appears to his doctor that such an application ought to be made. The patient will then be detained for observation or for

---

* Para 2.30.

19

treatment under section 25 or section 26 of the Act. Subsection (2) provides for the situation where a patient wishes to leave hospital before the application is completed. It may be used to prevent the patient leaving hospital where a patient becomes so disturbed on the ward that he seems to require restraint or treatment which could not be imposed on him as an informal patient. The doctor in charge of the patient's treatment may make a report to the managers informing them that he considers that an application for compulsory admission should be made, and this report then gives authority for the patient to be kept in hospital for up to 3 days whilst the necessary medical recommendations are obtained and the application completed.

2.30   At present the only person who can make the necessary report under section 30 is the doctor in charge of the patient's treatment and he is not always readily available. Delays occur during which nursing staff are unsure of their position in dealing with a patient who needs to be detained to prevent danger to himself or others. In attempts to avoid this, abuses sometimes occur. For example, a stock of forms which have already been signed by the doctor is sometimes kept ready for use when needed. This is obviously unsatisfactory, and the Consultative Document* suggested that a report by an experienced Registered Mental Nurse in conjunction with a doctor (not necessarily the doctor in charge of the patient's treatment) might be regarded as an adequate safeguard. Although there was general agreement on the need for change and for more flexibility, this suggestion received a mixed reaction. For the most part, medical opinion favoured widening the range of doctors who could sign reports and was against the involvement of nursing staff—largely on the grounds that it is inappropriate for nurses to be involved in medical decisions. Nursing opinion on the other hand generally favoured nursing involvement although some thought that this should be for only a very limited period.

2.31   In September 1977 the Confederation of Health Service Employees (COHSE) published a booklet on 'The Management of Violent or Potentially Violent Patients' highlighting, among other matters, the uncertainty which staff feel about their legal position in restraining an informal patient or in imposing treatment without the patient's consent. Action to prevent a patient causing injuries to others would seem to be justified in law under section 3(1) of the Criminal Law Act, 1967, which allows the use of such force as is reasonable in the circumstances in the prevention of crime. There is also a common law defence available to staff who act to prevent violence, to save life or in self-defence. However, there may be occasions when there is no actual emergency since violence has not yet arisen, but staff have good reason to believe that it is likely to do so. There may also be times when the behaviour of an informal patient requires physical control and he should clearly not be allowed to leave the ward or hospital, or where the danger of violence to others on the ward is such that short term seclusion seems essential.

*Proposal for a new 'holding power'*
2.32   In view of the conflicting reactions to the proposal in the Consultative Document for modifying section 30, an alternative is now put forward.

*Paras 2.17 to 2.19.

The main object is to minimise the time during which nursing staff are left uncertain of their legal position in, perhaps forcibly, detaining a patient. The Government therefore proposes that a Registered Mental Nurse should be able to invoke a 'holding power' for a period of not more than six hours to enable the necessary report under section 30 to be obtained from the doctor in charge of the patient's treatment or his nominated deputy. The holding power might be invoked by the completion of a formal document by the nurse concerned. If, in the event, the doctor decides not to make a section 30 report either because the situation has improved or because he does not consider detention necessary, the position would be similar in some respects to that which occurs when section 136 powers are used by the police but do not lead to compulsory admission to hospital. In order to ensure that the new power is not over-used or used inappropriately, it will be important for senior staff and hospital managers to ensure that the documents are properly completed and for them to monitor closely the use of the power.

**Periods of Detention for the Emergency Powers (Sections 29, 30, 135 and 136)**

2.33 Although some have suggested a reduction in the maximum periods of detention—presently 72 hours or 3 days—under sections 29, 135, 136 and 30, most comments agreed with the view expressed in the Consultative Document* that for practical reasons the existing periods were about right. The Government proposes that powers under sections 29, 135 and 136 should continue to extend for up to 72 hours.

2.34 The section 30(2) power is at present for '3 days' rather than for the 72 hours provided under sections 29, 135 and 136. The distinction is confusing and may be open to misinterpretation; it is thus proposed to bring the section 30 period into line with that of the other sections.

*Period of detention under section 25*

2.35 Paragraph 2.12 recommends that section 25 should be amended to give statutory backing to its use in practice as a short term treatment and assessment order. If this is accepted the duration of the order must, whilst being recognisably short term, be long enough to enable a reasonably large number of people to be treated under it without having to invoke the longer term section 26 order. The present 28-day period is thought to provide this balance and no change is proposed.

THE LONGER TERM POWERS

**Compulsory Powers for Longer-Term Admission (Section 26 and Section 60)**

2.36 Most patients are at present compulsorily admitted to hospital on a long-term basis either by an application for admission for treatment under section 26 of the Mental Health Act or, as a result of criminal proceedings, by a hospital order made by a court under section 60. In 1976, 800 people were admitted to hospital under section 26 and about 900 under section 60. (Section 60 and other powers which relate to mentally disordered offenders are also discussed in Chapter 5.)

---

* Para 3.2.

2.37   An application under section 26 may be made by the nearest relative or by a Mental Welfare Officer. It must be supported by two medical recommendations, one of which must be by a doctor 'approved' under section 28 of the Act as having special experience in the diagnosis or treatment of mental disorder. If practicable one of the doctors giving a recommendation should be previously acquainted with the patient. Only one of the recommendations may be made by a doctor from the admitting hospital. At present, the conditions which have to be satisfied are that—

i.   the patient is suffering from mental illness or severe subnormality, or that he is suffering from subnormality or psychopathic disorder and is under 21; and

ii.   the mental disorder is of a nature or degree which warrants detention in hospital for medical treatment; and

iii.   it is necessary, in the interests of the patient's own health or safety or for the protection of others, that he is detained.

A court may make a hospital order under section 60 in respect of an offender suffering from mental illness, severe subnormality, subnormality or psychopathic disorder no matter what his age, provided that the mental disorder is of a nature or degree which warrants detention in hospital and that it is satisfied having regard to all the circumstances that such an order is the best means of dealing with the offender. If the court does not also make a restriction order under section 65, the patient's position is then broadly the same as that of a patient detained under section 26, with minor exceptions discussed in paragraph 5.7 below. The four categories of mental disorder and their definitions were discussed in Chapter 1: possible changes in the requirements which govern admission and detention under sections 26 and 60 are examined below.

**Age Limits and Treatability**

2.38   The Consultative Document* questioned whether the age limit of 21 which now applies to the admission under section 26 of patients suffering from psychopathic disorder or subnormality should be retained. It pointed out that an age limit was arbitrary and led to anomalies, in that similar patients might be treated differently simply because of a slight age difference. The comments received showed strong support for the removal of age limits, and the Government proposes that they should be removed. This will mean that patients over 21 suffering from mental handicap or psychopathic disorder will come within the scope of section 26 (or guardianship under section 33) and alternative safeguards against unnecessary detention may be needed. The Consultative Document suggested that a section 26 order should not be made unless the doctor confirms that the patient is likely to benefit from treatment.

2.39   However precisely any requirement of a prospect of benefit from treatment is expressed in legislation, it will inevitably allow for admission of some mentally handicapped and psychopathic people over the age of 21 who cannot now be detained unless they commit an offence. On the other hand, the proposal (see paragraph 2.45 below) that renewal of

_____
* Paras 1.27 to 1.28.

detention should no longer be possible for these two groups unless there is a likelihood of benefit from treatment (even though grounds of health and safety or for the protection of others are satisfied) would mean that some people who are now liable to renewal of detention after the age of 21 will be free to leave hospital.

2.40 The Consultative Document* suggested that a 'benefit from treatment' requirement might apply to all four categories of mental disorder. However, there is the possibility that such a requirement would preclude the compulsory admission of some severely mentally handicapped people or of mentally ill persons suffering from illnesses who are unlikely to benefit from treatment in the sense that their condition may not improve; these people might nevertheless need to be admitted on occasions, for example, to tide them over a crisis. It is accordingly proposed that the requirement to certify a likelihood of benefit from treatment should apply on admission only to those suffering from mental handicap and psychopathic disorder (for whom it would replace the present age limit and for whom the need for medical and nursing care is more questionable), and not to the mentally ill or the severely mentally handicapped. This requirement is intended to apply to admissions of those suffering from mental handicap or psychopathic disorder under Part V of the Act (sections 60 and 72) as well as under section 26. The suggested arrangements for renewal of detention are discussed in paragraphs 2.43 and 2.45 below.

**Other Criteria for Admission and Detention**

2.41 At present the admission of a patient under section 26 (but not under section 60) must be 'in the interests of the patient's health or safety or for the protection of other persons'. The Consultative Document** discussed MIND's suggestion that compulsory admission should instead be related to 'dangerousness to self or others or to grave disablement'. This might however prevent treatment being given to people who need it but who do not represent a danger to others. The document suggested instead that the present requirement should continue in relation to admission but that a stricter criterion of 'dangerousness to self or others or grave disablement' might be required for renewal of detention if at that time the doctor in charge of the patient could not certify that there was a positive expectation of benefit from further treatment. The proposed retention of the existing criterion at the time of admission has been widely endorsed. Besides recognising the arguments put forward in the Consultative Document, some people have pointed out that making dangerousness a criterion for admission might increase the stigma often attaching to those detained under compulsory powers.

2.42 It is proposed to retain the existing requirement for admission but to amend the wording to make clearer the distinction between the patient's welfare and the protection of others. Thus the requirements might be reworded so that detention in hospital has to be necessary:

    a. in the interests of the health or safety of the patient *or*

    b. to protect others from harm.

---

\* Paras 1.27 to 1.28.

\*\* Paras 1.29 to 1.31.

This would continue to apply to all four categories of mental disorder and would be additional to the need, in the case of those suffering from mental handicap and psychopathic disorder, to certify the likelihood of benefit to the patient from the treatment proposed (paragraph 2.40 above).

*Criteria for renewal of detention*

2.43 The Consultative Document argued that it might be unreasonable to continue to use the criterion of the health or safety of the patient or the protection of others in deciding whether to detain a patient further after he had received a period of treatment. It suggested that, where the doctor could no longer certify that further treatment was likely to be beneficial, continued detention should be based on the stricter criterion of dangerousness to self or others or grave disablement. Most comments supported this, but some thought that the present broader criterion ought to remain. In exploring this further, it is necessary to discuss separately the considerations which apply to the mentally ill and severely mentally handicapped, and those which apply to the mentally handicapped and those suffering from psychopathic disorder.

2.44 By the end of an initial period of detention under section 26 (which, it is suggested in paragraph 2.47 below, should be a maximum of six months) it should be possible to assess whether a mentally ill or severely mentally handicapped patient is benefiting from treatment and is likely to continue to benefit; and it is proposed that the Responsible Medical Officer should be able to recommend renewal of detention on the grounds of the health or safety of the patient or protection of others only if he is also able to certify that there is likely to be benefit from further treatment. However, the health and social services authorities have a clear responsibility to care for the mentally ill and severely mentally handicapped and, where necessary, to protect the public from their actions. There will be a few cases where continued detention may be necessary but where there can be little expectation of treatment having any beneficial effect. In these cases the Government proposes that the patient should only have his detention renewed if—

   i. he is unable to maintain himself, even with help from his family or community services, or to protect himself from serious exploitation, (this might be termed 'grave incapacity'); or
   ii. there is a likelihood that he will cause serious harm to others.

2.45 Different arguments apply in relation to those suffering from mental handicap or psychopathic disorder where there is not the same need for medical and nursing care. Nor is the role of the Health Service as clear-cut for these groups, and it would be wrong to provide what would be no more than preventive detention. The Government therefore thinks that there should be a certification of likelihood of benefit from treatment both at admission and at renewal of detention for these two groups. With this proviso, the Government proposes to retain at renewal the broader criterion that continued detention is necessary in the interests of the health or safety of the patient or to protect others from harm. One effect will be that some people over the age of 21, at present detained but for whom there is no likelihood of benefit from treatment, will no longer be subject to renewal of detention.

### Number of Medical Recommendations

2.46    A possibility discussed in the Consultative Document* was that renewal of detention should, as with an application for admission for treatment under section 26, be based on the recommendations of two doctors instead of a report only from the Responsible Medical Officer. It was pointed out, however, that it might be difficult to obtain a second medical opinion which would be seen as truly independent; instead, better monitoring arrangements by Health Authorities were suggested to ensure that in each case there was a critical examination of the need for continued detention. Improved monitoring together with a requirement of a likelihood of benefit from treatment and automatic referrals to Tribunals (see paragraphs 7.3 and 7.4 below) should, the Government considers, provide sufficient extra safeguards.

### Periods of Detention under Sections 26 and 60

2.47    The Consultative Document suggested** that the present periods of detention under sections 26 and 60 (without restrictions) of one year followed by one more year and then two-yearly thereafter, should be halved to six months, followed by six more months, and then one year. This suggestion received overwhelming support, though MIND suggested that the initial detention period should be not more than 90 days and that renewal should be for not more than 120 days. It is thought however that three months may be too short a period to enable the Responsible Medical Officer to assess the effects of the treatment which is being provided, and it is therefore proposed to halve the present periods.

SUMMARY OF PROPOSALS: CHAPTER 2

*Section 29*

   i.  It is proposed to retain section 29 with the following changes:
       a.  It should be amended to provide for its use as a short 'cooling off' or assessment period in its own right (para 2.5).
       b.  Tighter monitoring of its use and of admission forms should be introduced (para 2.5).
       c.  The maximum period during which the applicant should personally have seen the patient should be reduced from 3 days to 24 hours and admission should take place within 24 hours of the medical examination or the application (whichever is the earlier) instead of 3 days (para 2.6).
       d.  Only the patient's nearest relative should be allowed to make an application, not any relative as at present (para 2.7).
       e.  Removal to a 'place of assessment' rather than to a hospital only should be provided for (para 2.8).
       f.  If compulsory powers in the community are introduced, it should be possible to convert an order under section 29 into a short term order in the community (para 2.8).

---

\* Paras 4.3 and 4.4.
\*\* Para 3.8.

*Section 25*

ii. It is proposed to retain section 25 with the following changes—

    a. It should explicitly provide for short term assessment and treatment (para 2.12).

    b. Admission should remain available for all forms of mental disorder. (But sexual deviancy, drug or alcohol dependence should not of themselves be regarded as mental disorder) (para 2.13).

    c. Section 25 applications should give fuller reasons and be more closely monitored (para 2.14).

    d. The nearest relative should have the same right to discharge a section 25 patient as for a section 26 patient (para 2.15).

    e. Where a section 25 patient requests a review by the hospital managers they must arrange for him to be interviewed within 3 days and give their decision within 7 days (para 2.16).

    f. The practicality of Mental Health Review Tribunal involvement in appeals against section 25 admission should be further investigated (para 2.17).

    g. It should be made clear that section 25 cannot be renewed (para 2.18).

*Sections 135 and 136*

iii. Section 135 should be retained and amended to provide also for cases where two mentally disordered people are living together and are unable to care for themselves (para 2.21).

iv. Section 136 should be retained and—

    a. guidance should make it clear that a police station should only be used as a 'place of safety' as a last resort (para 2.25).

    b. a form giving reasons for the use of the section should be devised and recommended in guidance (para 2.28).

*Section 30*

v. Section 30 should be retained but—

    a. should be amended so as to give an appropriately qualified nurse a 'holding power' for a period of up to 6 hours to enable a report to be obtained from either the doctor in charge of the patient's treatment or his nominated deputy (para 2.32).

    b. the period for which a patient can be detained under the section should be amended from '3 days' to 72 hours (para 2.34).

*Age limits and treatability*

vi. The age limit of up to 21 for compulsory admission of psychopaths and the mentally handicapped under section 26 should be removed, but there should be a requirement to certify that the patient 'is likely to benefit from treatment'. The requirement should also apply to Part V (sections 60 and 72) (paras 2.38 and 2.39).

vii. This 'treatability' requirement should not apply to the compulsory admission of the mentally ill or the severely mentally handicapped (para 2.40).

*Other criteria*

viii. The existing criterion for compulsory admission to hospital that it should be in the interests of the patient's health or safety or for the protection of others should be amended to—

*either* that it is in the interests of the health or safety of the patient
*or* that there is a need to protect others from harm
*and* for psychopaths and the mentally handicapped that there is a likelihood of benefit from treatment (para 2.42).

*Renewal of detention*

ix. The criteria for renewal of detention for all four groups should be—
  a. that it is necessary
      *either* in the interests of the health or safety of the patient
      *or* to protect others from harm.
  b. *and* that there is likely to be benefit from further treatment.
  c. for the mentally ill and severely mentally handicapped only, even when there is no likelihood of benefit from treatment, further detention should be possible on grounds of
      *either* grave incapacity
      *or* a likelihood that the patient will cause serious harm to others (paras 2.43 to 2.45).

x. Only one medical recommendation should continue to be required for renewal of detention (para 2.46).

*Periods of detention*

xi. The periods of detention for sections 26 and 60 should be halved to six months followed by another six months, then one year (para 2.47).

# CHAPTER 3

# ADMISSION PROCEDURES

**Introduction**

3.1  However fully legislation may spell out the criteria for the use of compulsory powers under the Mental Health Act and the safeguards against misuse, it is on the individuals invoking these powers that the burden of responsibility for proper use must largely rest. The responsibility is a heavy one in which the protection of the public and the importance of ensuring that mentally disordered people receive the help they need have to be weighed against the very serious step of deprivation of liberty. Admissions on a voluntary basis are of course desirable whenever possible; but when it is necessary to use compulsory powers, it is particularly important that the law is strictly observed. This is not always easy because the compulsory procedures are inevitably complex and moreover frequently have to be carried out in situations which are confused and distressing and where urgent action is imperative. They also involve people whose interests do not necessarily coincide. These may include, apart from the patient himself, Mental Welfare Officers, the police, the patient's relatives (who may themselves be under considerable stress), the health and social services authorities who have duties under the Act, and the staff who manage and provide services on their behalf.

3.2  In nearly all cases the law is no doubt scrupulously observed. However, there has recently been controversy over a few cases where it seems that powers may have been misused. Sometimes this has apparently occurred because of insufficient experience or training. In other cases, it seems that incorrect completion of applications—for example, applications signed by people not authorised to do so—have not been checked by staff in the admitting hospital.

**Doctors 'Approved' Under Section 28**

3.3  Section 28 of the Act specifies which doctors may make medical recommendations for an application for admission to hospital under sections 25 and 26. They should normally be a doctor who knows the patient (eg the family doctor) and a doctor 'approved' as having special experience in the diagnosis or treatment of mental disorder. Responsibility for approving doctors for this purpose rests with the Area Health Authority acting on the advice of a panel of psychiatrists.

3.4  At present, where two doctors' recommendations are needed (for sections 25 and 26), only one can be by a doctor employed at the receiving hospital, the intention being to ensure two quite independent opinions. The Consultative Document* discussed the problem in some areas of obtaining

---

* Paras 6.7 to 6.12.

recommendations from 'approved' doctors and suggested that the present rule might be relaxed to allow both medical recommendations to be made by doctors on the staff of the same hospital as long as one of them worked most of his sessions elsewhere. This suggestion was well received, and the Government proposes that it should be adopted.

3.5 One of the two medical recommendations needed before a court can make a hospital order under Part V of the Act must also be by a doctor approved under section 28(2); but there is no provision relating to the two doctors not being from the same hospital or institution. It seems undesirable, however, that either a court, in considering the disposal of an offender, or the Home Secretary, in considering a proposal for transfer to hospital under sections 72 or 73, should receive recommendations from two prison medical officers from the same prison, or from doctors working most of their time in the same hospital or institution, whether this is the receiving institution or not. The Government therefore proposes to incorporate a provision to prevent this: as far as prison medical officers are concerned, such a provision would formalise existing administrative practice. In the light of the comments made by the Butler Committee* the Government also proposes to apply to medical recommendations made under Part V of the Act the specific limitations on the relationship between the patient (and the applicant) and the doctors making the recommendations, and between the doctors themselves, which apply to Part IV applications.

3.6 The Government has also considered the Butler Committee's recommendation** that a medical recommendation in respect of a person who is mentally handicapped should be made by an 'approved' doctor who has special experience in the care and treatment of mental handicap. Making this a statutory requirement might however lead to practical difficulties, particularly in areas where there is a shortage of 'approved' doctors with the necessary specialist skills. It is thought preferable to regard the choice of a doctor with appropriate experience as a matter of good practice, and to cover this suggestion in guidance following amending legislation.

**The Role of the Mental Welfare Officer**

3.7 The Mental Welfare Officer replaced the 'duly authorised officer' when the Mental Health Act took effect in 1960. He has the important function of making an application for the admission of a mentally disordered person to hospital if the nearest relative does not wish to do so himself or if there is no nearest relative. It is the duty of a Mental Welfare Officer 'to make an application for admission to hospital or a guardianship application in respect of a patient within the area of the local authority by whom that Officer is appointed in any case where he is satisfied that such an application ought to be made and is of opinion, having regard to any wishes expressed by relatives of the patient or any other relevant circumstances, that it is necessary or proper for the application to be made by him'.

3.8 The Consultative Document*** recognised the doubts in some quarters about the role of the Mental Welfare Officer in admission procedures

---

\*    Cmnd 6244. Paras 14.2 to 14.4.

\*\*   Cmnd 6244. Para 14.6.

\*\*\* Paras 6.13 to 16.17.

but argued that this was largely due to the changes which have taken place in social work since 1959 and that legislative change is not required. It suggested that, as their training improves, Mental Welfare Officers will play a more positive role in assessing, on the basis of their social work expertise, whether compulsory hospital admission is needed or whether some alternative solution is preferable. It also suggested that a code of practice might be introduced to assist with some of the practical problems which have arisen in operating the relevant sections of the Act.

3.9 The comments received show that there is widespread concern about the lack of specialist knowledge on the part of many social workers engaged in mental health work; this has been attributed to the setting up of social services departments and the concept of the 'general purpose' social worker which arose from the Seebohm Report.* The criticisms are of course not all generally applicable; but there is no doubt that services for mentally disordered people are patchy and in some cases leave much to be desired. There is evidently a fairly general desire to reintroduce an element of specialisation to ensure that social workers responsible for making applications for compulsory admission have relevant experience and knowledge. Views varied as to the amount of experience and/or training required. Some have suggested that specialist training or qualification should be required, whilst others have suggested that Mental Welfare Officers should be required to be 'approved' in a similar way to doctors. The British Association of Social Workers (BASW) have suggested** that a central register be drawn up of social workers accredited with experience in the mental health field and that the professional association should be responsible for maintaining the register and admitting social workers to it.

3.10 The Government thinks that an arrangement whereby local social services authorities 'approve' Mental Welfare Officers in the light of guidance from professional and training bodies, much in the same way that health authorities 'approve' doctors under section 28, would be preferable to setting up and maintaining a central register. This would allow flexibility to take account of local variation and a gradual raising of standards over the years. It would require local social services authorities to appoint 'approved' Mental Welfare Officers for their locality on the basis of guidelines to be agreed in consultation with professional and training bodies and the local authority associations. The Government agrees with BASW that the title of 'Mental Welfare Officer' is out of date and should be changed to 'Approved Social Worker'.

3.11 Some of those commenting on the Consultative Document saw a need to define the duties of Mental Welfare Officers more closely and argued that there is some confusion about their role. BASW suggest*** that the role and duty of the Mental Welfare Officer should be—

'a. to investigate the patient's social situation and to identify, in consultation with others involved, the extent to which social and environmental pressures have contributed to his observed behaviour;

---

* Cmnd 3703. 'The Report of the Committee on Local Authority and Allied Social Services', HMSO (1968).
** 'Mental Health Crisis Services—A New Philosophy'. BASW Publications (1977) para 22.4.
*** Ibid. Paragraph 3.5.

b. to use his professional skills to help resolve any social relationship or environmental difficulties which have contributed to the crisis, and to mobilise community resources appropriately;

c. to be familiar with legal requirements, and to ensure that they are complied with;

d. to form his own opinions, following an interview with the patient, with those closest to him, and with others involved, as to whether compulsory admission is necessary having regard to any alternative methods of resolving the crisis, and of securing necessary care or treatment;

e. to ensure that care and treatment is offered in the least restrictive conditions possible.'

3.12 Whilst accepting that it would be of value to clarify what is expected of Mental Welfare Officers, this would probably be better done by way of guidance rather than legislation. It is proposed, however, that the Act and application forms should be amended to give the 'Approved Social Worker'—

i. a statutory duty to interview the person concerned before making an application for compulsory admission; and

ii. a responsibility to satisfy himself that the care and treatment offered is in the least restrictive conditions practicable in the circumstances.

3.13 The comments have indicated general agreement that a code of practice on admission procedures would be useful. It is recognised that it will not be an easy task to produce this, especially in relation to out-of-hours services when there are such marked differences in local circumstances. Co-operation between the professions concerned is essential, and it is proposed that the code should cover all the professions concerned and be included in the guidance to be issued following amending legislation.

**The Role of Relatives**

3.14 The nearest relative has, if he chooses to make use of the powers given to him by the Act, an important function in admission and discharge procedures. He can make an application for the patient to be admitted to hospital under sections 25 or 26 or to guardianship under section 33. An application for emergency admission under section 29 can at present be made by *any* relative. (In each case, the application may, alternatively, be made by a Mental Welfare Officer.)

3.15 The nearest relative also has the right, if an application for admission to hospital under section 26 or guardianship under section 33 is proposed by a Mental Welfare Officer, to notify that officer or his employing authority that he objects to such an application being made. His objection is then a bar save where, on an application made to it by a Mental Welfare Officer or any other person entitled to do so, a County Court decides that the objection is unreasonable.* In such a case the Court may make an order under section 52 appointing some other person to carry out the

---

* or that one of the other criteria listed under section 52(3) is satisfied.

functions of the nearest relative under the Act. The nearest relative may also order the discharge of the patient at any time during the currency of an order under sections 26 or 33. Where the patient is detained under section 26, the relative must, however, give 72 hours' written notice of his intention. If within that period the Responsible Medical Officer certifies to the Hospital Managers that in his opinion the patient, if released, would be likely to be dangerous to himself or others, the order of discharge is ineffective; but the nearest relative must be informed and may apply to a Mental Health Review Tribunal for the patient's discharge.

3.16 The question of the extent to which the nearest relative should continue to be formally involved in admission and discharge procedures was discussed in the Consultative Document*. One option considered was that the nearest relative's right to order discharge might be retained whilst removing his power to apply for compulsory admission. A substantial number of those commenting felt that applications should always be made by a Mental Welfare Officer. Most of the comments, however, suggested that relatives should retain their existing powers in relation to both admission and discharge. At present, the great majority of applications for compulsory admissions are made by Mental Welfare Officers. There are practical as well as emotional reasons why this should be so—relatives are unlikely to know the legal requirements or to have the necessary forms. Once a social worker is on the scene, most relatives probably prefer him to sign the application form. If the Act is to make it a statutory requirement for an 'approved' social worker to interview a person before an application for compulsory admission to hospital or to guardianship is made, the occasions on which a relative signs the application forms are likely to become even fewer. However, as the Consultative Document pointed out, some relatives may prefer to feel that they are in control of the situation, and they will be in the best position to judge when they are unable to cope any longer with the patient. The Government thinks that the nearest relative's powers should be retained, but considers that the power in relation to section 29 which enables any relative to make an application is too wide. It proposes that, as with applications under sections 25, 26 and 33, only the nearest relative or the Mental Welfare Officer should be able to make such an application. No change is proposed in the nearest relative's right to prevent an admission under section 26 or reception into guardianship under section 33. The power of the nearest relative to order discharge is also felt to be a useful safeguard which should be retained; paragraph 2.15, above, proposes that this should be extended to patients detained under section 25.

3.17 It is also felt that there would be advantage in amending section 49 to incorporate the provision in section 39 of the Northern Ireland Mental Health Act whereby the 'nearest relative' is defined as the first person in a specified list of relatives 'who is caring for the patient, or who was so immediately before the admission of the patient'. With this change, there would be little point in retaining the provision that the nearest relative should ordinarily be resident in the UK, and it is proposed that this should

* Paras 6.3 to 6.6.

be repealed. It has been pointed out that section 49, in giving precedence to a father over a mother, may be at variance with the spirit of the Sex Discrimination Act, 1975. The Government therefore proposes to bring together categories (c)—'father'—and (d)—'mother'—in the hierarchy which determines who is the nearest relative in the same way as other categories which refer to both male and female relatives. Very often there will not be a need to distinguish between them, and where the patient has been living with only one of the parents, the proposal to bring the Act into line with Northern Ireland legislation would mean that that parent would be recognised as the nearest relative.

## The Role of Health Authorities and Social Services Authorities

3.18   Area Health Authorities, as 'managers' of mental illness and mental handicap hospitals, or social services authorities where persons have been admitted to guardianship, are responsible for ensuring that the proper procedures are carried out in relation to detention and discharge and that the necessary forms are correctly completed when a person is compulsorily detained in hospital or admitted to guardianship. Section 47 of the Act also empowers health authorities to discharge unrestricted detained patients and social services authorities to discharge persons subject to guardianship. Regulations allow an authority to delegate most of these functions to officials, but discharge can only be ordered by three or more members of the authority, or by three or more members of a committee or sub-committee authorised for that purpose by the authority. Not all the members of such a committee or sub-committee need to be members of the authority.

3.19   The Government regards the efficient performance of these functions as an important safeguard for patients. Information from Area Health Authorities about how they carry out these duties shows that practice varies widely both in terms of the method used (some authorities appoint a small specialist committee whilst other appoint all members) and of the extent to which the managers take an active part in discussing applications for discharge or for renewal of detention with the patients, doctors and other professionals. A small committee or sub-committee which can build up expertise and confidence in taking the necessary and sometimes difficult decisions seems more likely to play a positive role. The Government therefore intends to issue guidance recommending authorities to set up committees or sub-committees specifically for the purpose of carrying out the functions laid on authorities by the Act.

3.20   Some recent cases have indicated that forms are not always checked as thoroughly or as promptly as they should be. Authorities will also be asked to designate an officer to scrutinise forms as soon as practicable after they have been completed and to take any necessary action if they have been improperly completed. Primary responsibility must remain, however, with those who complete the forms on admission or renewal of detention. This task can be learned only with training and guidance from more experienced staff.

3.21   Ensuring that applications are correctly completed is, however, only one aspect. It is also important to ensure that the reasons given for compulsory admission and detention are carefully drawn in relation to each individual patient and do not become stereotyped, Earlier in this Paper it has been suggested that compulsory admission forms should give fuller reasons than they do now and that these should be closely scrutinised (paragraphs 2.5, 2.14, 2.28 and 2.46). This would seem an appropriate function for the committees referred to in paragraph 3.19, above, since they would have power to discharge the patient or person under guardianship if, after discussion with those involved, they were not satisfied that sufficient reasons had been put forward. It is proposed to include an appropriate reference to this in guidance following the amendment of the Act.

3.22   It is proposed (see paragraph 2.16) to establish a formal procedure whereby a detained patient not subject to a restriction order will have the right to ask the managers to exercise their power of discharge, and, in such cases the managers will be required to arrange for him to be interviewed on their behalf within 3 days and to give their decision within 7 days. In view of the short time limits, and of the Government's hope that the new arrangements will lead to better use of their powers of discharge, managers will need to establish clear procedures to be followed. In the guidance to be issued following amendment of the Act, it will be suggested that either an officer (perhaps the Sector Administrator) or a member of the appropriate committee or sub-committee of the Authority should be designated as the person responsible for conducting these interviews on behalf of managers and making the necessary report.

SUMMARY OF PROPOSALS: CHAPTER 3

*Section 28 doctors*

i.   Section 28 should be amended so that, where two medical recommendations are required, they may both be provided by doctors on the staff of the same hospital, so long as one of them works most of his sessions elsewhere (para 3.4).

ii.   The medical recommendations required by a Court before a hospital order can be made under Part V of the Act should not be from two doctors working for the majority of their time in the same prison or institution. The limitations which apply to medical recommendations under Part IV should be extended to Part V recommendations (para 3.5).

iii.   It should be urged in guidance that wherever possible the approved doctor making a recommendation for admission under sections 26, 60 or 72 should have special experience in the particular form of disorder from which the person is suffering (para 3.6).

*Mental Welfare Officers*

iv.   Local authorities should 'approve' Mental Welfare Officers in much the same way that health authorities 'approve' doctors under section 28 (para 3.10).

v.   The title 'Mental Welfare Officer' should be changed to 'Approved Social Worker' (para 3.10).

vi.   The 'Approved Social Worker' should have a statutory duty to interview a person before making an application for compulsory admission and satisfy himself that the care and treatment offered is in the least restrictive conditions practicable in the circumstances (para 3.12).

## The Role of Relatives

vii.  The nearest relative's power to apply for compulsory admission should be retained; only the nearest relative, and not any relative as at present, should have the right to make an application under section 29 (para 3.16).

viii.  The power of the nearest relative to order discharge should be retained and extended to patients detained under section 25 (para 3.16).

ix.  Section 49 should be amended so that the nearest relative is defined as the first in a list of relatives to be caring for the person concerned or to be doing so immediately before his admission (para 3.17).

x.  The provision that the nearest relative should ordinarily be resident in the UK should be repealed (para. 3.17).

xi.  A single category 'parent' should replace 'father' and 'mother' in section 49 (para 3.17).

## The Role of Health Authorities and Social Services Authorities

xii.  Authorities should be asked to establish special committees or sub-committees to carry out the functions laid on them by the Act (para 3.19).

xiii.  They should also be asked to designate an officer to scrutinise application forms and to take the necessary action if they are not properly completed (para 3.20).

xiv.  Applications for admission and renewal of detention should be monitored by the committees or sub-committees (para 3.21).

xv.  A formal procedure should be established whereby managers designate an officer or member to interview within 3 days a patient who has applied for discharge and for the authority to give its decision in 7 days (para 3.22).

# CHAPTER 4

# GUARDIANSHIP AND COMPULSORY POWERS
# IN THE COMMUNITY

## Guardianship

4.1   The guardianship powers are contained in sections 33 and 60 of the 1959 Act. Under section 33 an application for guardianship can be made in respect of a person who is suffering from mental illness or severe subnormality whatever his age or of a person who is under the age of 21 and suffering from subnormality or psychopathic disorder. Section 60 empowers a court to place an offender suffering from mental disorder under guardianship on his conviction of an offence*; no age limits apply.

4.2   An application under section 33 has to be either in the interests of the person concerned or to protect others, and for both sections 33 and 60 the nature or degree of the disorder has to be such as to warrant reception into guardianship. The period of guardianship is initially one year, but renewable for a further year and thereafter at 2 yearly intervals. A local social services authority or a person approved by the authority can be named as guardian: the guardian must consent to being appointed.

4.3   MIND,** the Royal College of Psychiatrists and the Butler Committee*** have all suggested that more use should be made of guardianship. It is felt that guardianship may be a useful alternative to detention in hospital or more effective for some offenders than a probation order. It has also been suggested that it would be possible to discharge some patients from hospital earlier if there were powers for compulsory supervision or after-care following discharge. The British Association of Social Workers (BASW)**** have also recently put forward a proposal that  new type of compulsory order—which they have suggested might be called a 'community care order'—should be introduced.

4.4   The common thread running through these suggestions is that the care and treatment of the mentally disordered might be improved if compulsory powers did not begin and end at the hospital door. The argument seems to be that if hospital and community services are to be fully integrated and if coercive powers are needed in some cases then these cannot logically be confined to only part of the integrated service. These questions raise important issues; the Government's provisional view is set out in this chapter; further public debate and consultation are needed, and comments on the proposals outlined below would be welcomed.*****

---

\*        In certain circumstances, a magistrates' court may make such an order without convicting (section 60(2)).

\*\*      'A Human Condition'. Vol I, p. 64.

\*\*\*    Cmnd 6244. Chapter 15.

\*\*\*\*  'Mental Health Crisis Services—A New Philosophy'. Para 4.

\*\*\*\*\* Views on these proposals should be forwarded to the Secretary, Interdepartmental Committee on the Review of the Mental Health Act 1959, Room C421, Department of Health and Social Security, Alexander Fleming House, London SE1 6BY

## The Royal Commission 1954-7

4.5 The existing guardianship powers are based on recommendations in the Report of the 'Royal Commission on the Law relating to Mental Illness and Mental Deficiency 1954-57'* (paragraphs 387, 399, 400, 411). The Royal Commission argued that care outside hospital should usually be on the basis of persuasion to accept help and advice and take advantage of arrangements for employment or training. However, the Commission recommended that where a person's unwillingness to receive training or social help could not be overcome by persuasion it would appropriate to place him under guardianship if this offered the prospect of success. The Commission suggested that care under guardianship might be more appropriate for some people, particularly those with mild or chronic forms of mental illness, than compulsory admission to or continued detention in hospital.

4.6 The Royal Commission recommended (in paragraph 387) that local authorities should have a duty to accept the responsibilities of guardianship whenever there were no other suitable guardians. It also recommended short-term guardianship powers in cases of emergency not requiring admission to hospital. The Commission recommended that in such cases guardianship powers should be exercisable for up to 28 days, extended where necessary by completion of the normal precedure. Neither recommendation was, however, enacted.

## Practice since 1959

4.7 The use of guardianship powers has declined steadily since their introduction and practice varies considerably between local authorities. The Royal Commission expected that as community psychiatric services developed guardianship would become more frequent, but this hope has not been borne out. Nor has their hope that guardianship would be used for the mentally ill and psychopaths. In practice, guardianship has been used predominantly for the mentally handicapped and the severely mentally handicapped and only very rarely for the mentally ill.

4.8 There are probably many reasons for this but one may be the nature of guardianship powers and doubts about what is involved in exercising them. As suggested by the Royal Commission and embodied in section 34 (1) of the Mental Health Act 1959 the guardian has the powers of a father over a child under 14. Such powers are nowhere specified in detail. Regulations** lay down that 'The guardian shall, so far as if practicable, make arrangements for the occupation, training or employment of the patient and for his recreation and general welfare and shall ensure that everything practicable is done for the promotion of his physical and mental health'. One widely used legal reference argues that persons under guardianship cannot marry; and the Butler Committee*** commented that those under guardianship cannot make a valid legal contract. Although not all lawyers take the same view, the power is undoubtedly a wide one and it seems that some authorities feel that a guardian must necessarily exercise

---

*    Cmnd 169. HMSO (1957).
**   SI 1960/1241. Para 6.
*** Cmnd 6244. Para 15.2.

'parental' powers in a broad sense and must accept extensive responsibility for the behaviour and protection of the person concerned. Such a view naturally leads to a use of guardianship primarily in those cases—such as the severely mentally handicapped—where there is need to protect the individual from neglect and exploitation and to make most, if not all, of his decisions. It may have led to guardianship not being considered—as the Commission hoped it might be—as a way of reducing unwillingness to accept help and as a way of providing supervision, guidance and control which would be a real alternative to detention in hospital.

### BASW's proposal

4.9  BASW* have argued that the admission of people to psychiatric hospitals should be regarded as a last resort. In particular, they saw it as undesirable to admit people to hospital simply because of a lack of services in the community, or because of the lack of appropriate powers. They have suggested that as well as existing guardianship powers there should be a new range powers, to be known as community care orders, which would parallel existing compulsory hospital powers. They propose that local social services authorities should have a responsibility to provide care for and to control persons made subject to community care orders, and that this responsiblity should be exercised on the authority's behalf only by social workers approved for the purpose as having had the requisite training and experience. BASW suggest that power under a community care order should be comparable to that of the existing power over a detained patient on leave from hospital. This power is a broad one and is set out in section 39(1) of the Mental Health Act; it allows the Responsible Medical Officer to impose 'such conditions (if any) as that officer considers necessary in the interests of the patient or for the protection of other persons.'

4.10  It is clearly preferable that, as with hospital treatment, community care should be accepted voluntarily by those who need it and that compulsory care should be regarded as a last resort, to be adopted only when all efforts of persuasion have failed. In the absence of such powers persons needing care and control may be faced with perhaps unnecessary detention in a hospital. It is this 'gap' in the range of alternatives that forms the basis of BASW's argument.

4.11  A similar argument applies to the after-care of persons detained in hospital who could be discharged if there were community powers of supervision and control. The Butler Committee conclusion in Chapter 8 of their Report was against compulsory after-care. Instead they commended trial leave from hospital (under section 39) in appropriate cases. Section 39 however permits the patient to be given leave only for 6 months and if during this period the patient has not returned to hospital the authority for his detention lapses. In some cases, where longer supervision is needed, the patient is brought back to hospital at the end of the 6 months' period for an overnight stay in the hospital, simply in order to authorise a further 6 months' period of 'trial leave'. This is a misuse of the powers; and some doctors feel that it would be useful to be able to provide a much longer

---

* *'Mental Health Crisis Services—A New Philosophy'*. Para 11.2

period of compulsory supervision in the community. The Royal Commission saw such supervision as one of the appropriate uses of guardianship. MIND* went further than the Butler Committee and suggested that a power of compulsory after-care should be introduced at the discretion of the discharging authority, subject to a maximum period of one year. MIND feel that, without a provision of this kind, a restriction order might be imposed by the court simply to ensure after-care and supervision. MIND also saw compulsory after-care as a preferable alternative to what otherwise might amount to preventive detention. Mental Health Review Tribunals sometimes decide against discharging a patient because they think he needs supervision after discharge and are not convinced that he would comply with arrangements on a voluntary basis. The suggestion that Tribunals should have power to make conditional discharges is discussed in paragraph 6.5, below. The Government's view is that it would be preferable to recommend compulsory supervision in the community. It would seem sensible to have a single power for compulsory supervision intended to prevent unnecessary admission to hospital and for compulsory after-care following discharge from hospital.

4.12 Proposals for compulsory powers outside hospital are open to a number of objections. There would be no satisfactory sanctions in the event of the patient's failure to comply with the requirements laid on him and it is feared that social services staff might be unwilling to take on the responsibilities involved in new compulsory powers or might be unable to take on the burden of extra commitments. The introduction of additional powers might also significantly increase the number of people made subject to compulsory powers of one kind or another. Moreover, there might be a danger that in difficult or emergency circumstances compulsion would be used without full exploration of the alternatives. The new powers would normally be exercised by social workers or community psychiatric nurses. Some doctors may have reservations about backing such action; they may take the view that people who are so disordered as to need to be compelled to submit to care should be admitted to hospital. The number of people whom the new powers might benefit seems likely to be limited. The use of the powers will depend upon the ability of social services staff to take on the work and responsibilities involved. This ability will be restricted by the lack of suitable experience and training of some social services staff and, of course, the development of the manpower resources needed will be dependent upon economic circumstances. There is therefore unlikely to be a significant increase in the number of people made subject to compulsory powers. The lack of an effective sanction can be said to apply to most forms of compulsory detention in hospital at present, particularly where 'open door' policies are fully operative. The Royal Commission pointed out that the possession of a formal authority of itself is sometimes sufficient to obtain co-operation which might otherwise not be given. In some cases, the sanction against non-compliance with a community care order would be compulsory detention in hospital, but this of course would only be where detention for treatment was warranted and when the other criteria for compulsory detention were met.

---

* 'A Human Condition'. Vol 2, pp. 42–5.

4.13   The Government believes that powers of compulsion of some kind are needed for a small minority of people; it has however reached no firm conclusions on what these powers should be. Clearly the freedom and rights of individuals should be restricted as little as possible. The development of mental health services in the next few decades, as envisaged in the 'Better Services' White Papers*, involves building up local networks of health and social services with an emphasis on community based patterns of care and after-care. Changes in the nature of compulsory powers should be in keeping with these ideas. The following paragraphs discuss the options that seem open.

**Option (i): Guardianship in a Revised Form**

4.14   One option is to retain existing guardianship powers in more or less their present form, but with some minor changes. BASW, in proposing community care orders, made the point that guardianship powers meet the needs of some people for extensive protective support. It needs to be made clear that the role of the guardian is to protect the person from exploitation and harm. One of the criteria for admission to guardianship could also be more strictly defined. At present an application under section 33 has to be 'necessary in the interests of the patient or for the protection of other persons'.** This criterion seems unnecessarily wide and the term 'patient's welfare' in place of 'patient' would help to narrow it. The guardian would continue to have power to consent to treatment on the patient's behalf, but the special arrangements for a second opinion in relation to certain treatments (paras 6.14—6.30) would apply. There seems no reason why a relative or friend, subject to the approval of the appropriate local social services authority, should not continue to exercise guardianship powers where appropriate; and indeed why a relative should not make an application for guardianship powers. It is proposed however that applications should have the support of a social worker with approved experience and be based upon the written recommendations of two medical practitioners.

4.15   The Consultative Document suggested*** that removal of age limits for compulsory hospital admissions would need to be accompanied by an equivalent change in guardianship provisions. Most comments agreed and it is proposed that this should be done. The Document also suggested that the periods of guardianship should be reduced in line with the periods of hospital orders. This has also been generally agreed; and it is proposed that the currency of guardianship powers should be 6 months, renewable for a further 6 months and thereafter renewable annually. It is also proposed to make provision for automatic Tribunal reviews of guardianship in line with hospital orders (paragraph 6.3 below). Guardianship powers would be improved if modified in this way but even then would not be very suitable for people whose need is for care or after-care under controlled conditions rather than for overall protection.

---

*   Cmnd 4683. 'Better Services for the Mentally Handicapped';
            Cmnd 6233. 'Better Services for the Mentally Ill'.
**   This criterion does not apply under section 60.
*** Para 5.6.

## Option (ii): Community Care Orders

4.16   A second option is to adopt the suggestion in paragraph 4.9, above, for a range of community care orders paralleling compulsory hospital powers. The Government finds this an interesting proposal and of course has sympathy with the desire to avoid unnecessary hospital admission. However, the extent of control which community care orders would entail is so wide that this option might well suffer from the same disadvantages as guardianship has in the past.

## Option (iii): 'Essential Powers' Approach

4.17   A third option is to introduce new specific powers limited to restricting the liberty of the individual only to the extent necessary to ensure that various forms of medical treatment, social support, training or occupation are undertaken. Under this option a social services authority would have specific powers:

   i. to require residence in a specified place;
   ii. to require attendance at specified places for treatment, occupation or training;
   iii. to require access to be given to a particular person (for instance, a doctor or a social worker) in the patient's home or elsewhere.

The grounds on which an application for these specific powers could be made, the method of application and the duration of the powers would be similar to those in respect of existing guardianship powers. Additionally, the courts might be empowered, on convicting an offender, to make an order conferring these powers on a social services authority, provided that the authority is prepared to accept the responsibility.

4.18   It is for consideration whether, in addition to the above powers, it would be desirable to have power to impose treatment on people subject to such an order under the same arrangements as those for people detained compulsorily in hospital (paragraphs 6.14 to 6.30 below). Where, for instance, a person could remain in the community if he were willing to accept maintenance on drugs, he must at present be compulsorily detained in hospital before his refusal to accept such treatment (except in an emergency) can be overridden. The Government would welcome views on this.

## Short Term Powers

4.19   Although the Royal Commission recommended the introduction of a short term form of guardianship lasting for 28 days, the Act only provides for long term powers. Should more specific guardianship powers on the lines suggested in para 4.17, above, be introduced, short term powers may be appropriate in some cases; for example, where treatment at a day hospital or as an outpatient was required. It would seem useful to be able to introduce a short term order to provide for an initial period of up to 28 days in which the guardian would be able to invoke the 3 essential powers listed in paragraph 4.17, above, after which the patient might be willing to co-operate and to continue treatment voluntarily or might no longer be in need of treatment. Longer term powers would remain the usual method and short-term powers would be available only under Part IV of the Act. Views are

41

sought on whether a short term order would be of value. The same safe-guards would apply as for section 25 orders (see paragraphs 2.14 and 2.15, above).

### 'Protective' Powers as an Addition

4.20   If option (iii), 'essential powers', (paras. 4.17 and 4.18) were adopted, there may still be a few people for whom additional 'protective' powers might be required. For example, for a person who has little or no understanding the wide guardianship powers, amended as described in paragraphs 4.14 and 4.15, above, would be needed to enable the guardian to consent to or refuse treatment, arrange admission to hospital etc where necessary on his behalf. There would thus be two different powers for two different groups of people. Similarly, if compulsory care orders (para 4.16 above) were introduced, existing guardianship powers could be retained to provide flexibility.

### Duties of Local Authorities

4.21   BASW has also advocated* adopting the suggestion of the Royal Commission that local authorities should have a duty to assume the responsibilities of guardianship whenever there are no other suitable guardians. The Government considers, however, that local authorities must be free to assess the desirability of their assuming compulsory powers in the light of their knowledge of each individual case, and no change in the law in this respect is proposed.

### SUMMARY OF PROPOSALS: CHAPTER 4

   a.  The Government invites views on three main options:

     *Option (i)*

     To retain existing guardianship powers, but to define them more clearly, to remove the present age limits and reduce the periods of guardianship in line with those for hospital orders (paras. 4.14 and 4.15).

     *Option (ii)*

     To introduce community care orders paralleling compulsory hospital orders (para. 4.16).

     *Option (iii)*

     To introduce new and more limited specific powers (paras. 4.17 and 4.18).

   b.b.  Possible alternatives are a combination of (i) and (ii), and a combination of (i) and (iii) (para. 4.20).

   c.  Two other points on which views are invited are whether the powers to impose treatment without consent should apply to the 'essential powers' approach if introduced (para 4.18) and whether a short-term community order should be introduced (para 4.19).

---

* *'Mental Health Crisis Services—A New Philosophy'*. Para 4.1.

CHAPTER 5

# OFFENDER PATIENTS

**Introduction**

5.1   This chapter discusses Part V of the Mental Health Act which concerns admission to hospital following criminal court proceedings, the Home Secretary's powers with regard to restricted patients and the transfer of certain categories of mentally disordered prisoners to hospital. The changes proposed have been stimulated mainly by the recommendations made by the Butler Committee and by volume 2 of *'A Human Condition'*, MIND's special report on the law relating to mentally abnormal offenders. The latter was published some 6 months after the Consultative Document and some of the issues it raised were not discussed either in the Butler Report or in the Consultative Document.

5.2   The last 10 years have seen a steady decline in the numbers of offenders compulsorily admitted to hospital. In 1966, 1,440 hospital orders were made by courts under section 60 of the Mental Health Act, whereas in 1976 there were only 924. This seems in part to be due to an increasing reluctance to admit offender patients to local hospitals. The Government is concerned about the difficulties this creates for the courts and prisons and for offenders whose mentally disordered condition warrants detention in hospital for treatment but who may have to be sent to or kept in prison rather than in hospital, for want of a suitable hospital place.

5.3   There seem to be several reasons for local hospitals' reluctance to receive mentally disordered offenders. The changes and developments which have taken place in the psychiatric services over the last 20 years are undoubtedly an important factor. During this period there has been a continuing move away from the concept of long-term custodial care of patients, and of many being compulsorily detained, to a more open therapeutic environment in which the vast majority of the patients admitted are 'informal' and short-stay. These changes have been of immense benefit to patients in general and to hospital staff. The changes have, however, led to a situation where staff seem to have become increasingly reluctant to assume responsibility for treating patients who are, or whom it is feared may be, disruptive or violent. Sometimes staff feel that they cannot offer appropriate treatment to the patient whilst in other cases there may be concern about whether the hospital has sufficient staff or facilities to provide proper security. The problem is sometimes increased when the court has added a restriction order under section 65. Some doctors feel that their hands are too much tied by these restrictions, the effect of which is to require them to seek the Home Secretary's consent before allowing a patient out of hospital for any period or discharging or transferring him; it can also lead to a situation where they may have to continue to take responsibility for a patient for whom they feel they can offer no further treatment.

5.4   The establishment of regional secure psychiatric units, as was recommended by the Butler Committee in their interim report* and also by a DHSS Working Party, will help. When established, these units will offer a degree of security less than that of the Special Hospitals but greater than that of the ordinary psychiatric hospitals and should be able to admit, amongst other groups, some mentally disordered offenders for whom courts are unable at present to obtain hospital places. It would be wrong, however, to regard them as offering anything like a complete solution to the problem; it will also be necessary to improve co-operation between the courts and hospitals.

5.5   In volume 2 of *'A Human Condition'***, MIND proposed that courts might be empowered to compel an Area Health Authority to admit an offender patient to hospital. They thought that it should be possible for the court, not to substitute its judgement for that of the AHA, but rather to be able to override a decision not to admit an offender if it were made without reasonable ground or in bad faith. The Government shares MIND's concern about the difficulties courts are currently experiencing in dealing with offenders whose mental condition is such that their condition warrants detention in hospital for treatment but does not believe that it would be realistic to look to a legislative solution. Courts will, in any case, be unlikely to be in a position to judge whether an AHA is acting unreasonably since this would involve a knowledge of the facilities and staffing resources available. It is hoped that the proposals made in paragraphs 5.30 to 5.34, below, for giving the receiving hospital an opportunity to express its views on the making of a restriction order will go some way towards improving co-operation between courts and hospitals.

## ORDERS UNDER SECTION 60

5.6   Under section 60, where a person is convicted before the Crown Court of an offence other than murder, or is convicted by a magistrates' court of an offence punishable on summary conviction with imprisonment, the court may make a hospital order as an alternative to an ordinary penal disposal such as imprisonment or a fine. The following three conditions must be satisfied. Firstly, the court must be satisfied on the evidence of two doctors (at least one with special knowledge of psychiatry) that the offender is suffering from one of the four categories of mental disorder specified in the Act and that the disorder is of a nature or degree which warrants detention in hospital for medical treatment. Secondly, the court must be of the opinion, 'having regard to all the circumstances including the nature of the offence and the character and antecedents of the offender, and to the other available methods of dealing with him', that the making of a hospital order is the most suitable method of disposing of the case. Thirdly, the court must be satisfied that arrangements have been made for the admission of the offender to a specified hospital within a period of 28 days.

---

* Cmnd 5698. *'Interim Report of the Committee on Mentally Abnormal Offenders'*. HMSO (1974).

** Pp 42-57, in particular pp 54 and 55.

5.7  A hospital order enables an offender to be admitted to, and compulsorily detained in, a hospital for treatment for as long as is necessary in the interests of his own health or safety or for the protection of other persons. In making the order the court is placing the patient in the hands of the doctors, foregoing any question of punishment and relinquishing from then onwards its own control over him. Except where restrictions have been imposed under section 65, the offender, on his admission to hospital, is placed in broadly the same position as a non-offender admitted on an application for treatment under section 26. The only differences are that the nearest relative has no right to order his discharge, and that the age limits which at present apply to the admission and detention of patients suffering from psychopathic disorder or subnormality do not apply. The hospital order, like an application for treatment under section 26, lasts initially for a period of one year and is subject to the same renewal arrangements. The patient can be discharged at any time by his doctor, the hospital managers, or by a Mental Health Review Tribunal to which the patient and his nearest relative have periodic rights to apply for his discharge. A number of proposals for amendment of section 60 and related provisions have already been considered in earlier parts of this Paper (paras 2.40, 2.45, 2.47 and 3.5, above; for convenience, these proposals are summarised at the end of this Chapter).

5.8  The only remaining point is that BASW* have suggested that it should be mandatory for courts to call for social enquiry reports since at present hospital orders may be made on the basis of medical evidence alone. It is, however, the usual practice of courts to call for social enquiry reports when asking for the necessary medical recommendations to be submitted. There does not seem to be a need to legislate on this point though a suitable opportunity will be taken to bring this matter formally to the attention of the courts.

## Guardianship orders

5.9  Section 60 also empowers a court to make a guardianship order in certain circumstances. The conditions which have to be satisfied before a person can be made subject to such an order are broadly similar to those for a hospital order. Guardianship orders are very rarely made by courts; in 1976, only 4 were made. Guardianship under section 60 means that the offender is subject to the same compulsory powers in the community as if he had been committed to guardianship under Part IV of the Act. The Government's proposals for amendment of guardianship powers are discussed in Chapter 4; except where otherwise indicated, the same considerations may be taken to apply to offenders as to non-offenders.

## RESTRICTION ORDERS UNDER SECTION 65

5.10  Section 65 provides that where a hospital order under section 60 is made by the Crown Court, and it appears to the Court, having regard to the nature of the offence, the antecedents of the offender, and the risk of his committing further offences if set at large, that it is necessary for the protection of the public to do so, the Court may further order that

---

* 'Mental Health Crisis Services—a New Philosophy'. Para 24.

the offender shall be subject to special restrictions either without limit of time or during such period as may be specified. A restriction order may not be made unless one of the doctors giving medical evidence for the purposes of making the hospital order has given oral evidence. The number of restriction orders made by the courts reached a peak in the early 1970s and now appears to be declining. Thus, in 1966 181 restriction orders were made. The figure for 1971 was 232, and for 1976 only 151.

5.11　The effect of a restriction order is that the patient cannot be discharged from hospital, transferred to another hospital or given leave of absence without the consent of the Home Secretary. The patient cannot apply directly to a Mental Health Review Tribunal for discharge but the Home Secretary may at any time refer his case to a Tribunal for advice, and must do so at certain intervals where requested by the patient. The Home Secretary is not, however, bound to accept the advice given him by the Tribunal. In authorising the discharge of a restricted patient, the Home Secretary may impose conditions, eg that the patient maintain contact with a social worker or probation officer. He also has power to recall to hospital at any time a patient who has been conditionally discharged from hospital and who remains liable to the special restrictions.

5.12　The Butler Committee* made the following suggestions for amendment of section 65 and related provisions—

  i. the section should be reworded to indicate what the Butler Committee regarded as the essential purpose of restriction orders, namely, to protect the public from serious harm (recommendation 108);

  ii. the present power of a court to make a restriction order of limited duration should be removed (recommendation 109);

  iii. an annual report should be submitted to the Home Secretary by the Responsible Medical Officer in respect of each restricted patient (recommendation 114);

  iv. there should be a statutory requirement to obtain the consent of the receiving consultant before a restriction order can be made by a court (recommendation 107); and

  v. where the supervising officer of a conditionally discharged restricted patient is of the opinion that the patient's behaviour is such that he should be recalled to hospital, but no place is immediately available, the Home Secretary should be able to authorise emergency admission to a 'place of safety' for up to 72 hours (recommendation 118).

5.13　The Consultative Document** suggested that the first three recommendations seemed acceptable but that the fourth should be rejected; it was argued that instead the scope for administrative action should be explored with a view to encouraging co-operation and consultation between receiving doctors and the courts in decisions to impose restriction orders. It also recommended rejection of the fifth suggestion***. Since the publication

---

*　Cmnd 6244. Paras 14.20 to 14.32.
**　Paras 10.17 to 10.21.
***　Paras 10.22 to 10.25.

of the Consultative Document MIND have published (in February, 1977) the second volume of their special report on the Mental Health Act, entitled *'A Human Condition'*, which included detailed observations on and proposals for amendment of section 65.

## Rewording of section 65

5.14    The Butler Committee* took the view that, because of their potentially serious consequences for patients, and less importantly because of the administrative difficulties they involve, restriction orders should only be made in really serious cases. Evidence they received from the Home Office indicated the probability that these orders were imposed in numbers of cases where their severity was not appropriate. The Committee considered that, although there had been a decline over recent years in the number of cases in which restriction orders had been imposed in relation to comparatively minor offences, the fact that the wording of section 65 contains no reference to the seriousness of the offences from which the public is intended to be protected means that some courts have inappropriately imposed restrictions—for example, on a petty recidivist on the ground that he would persist in offending. The Committee therefore recommended that the wording of the section should be more tightly drawn to indicate its true intention, namely, to protect the public from serious harm. MIND** also have cited a number of examples where restriction orders have been imposed in respect of relatively minor offences.

5.15    There can be little doubt that restriction orders have been imposed on occasions where they are not really justified by the nature of the offence or by the offender's previous criminal and medical history and hence that the wording of section 65 does give courts a rather wider discretion than was originally envisaged by the Royal Commission***. The Government therefore proposes that the wording of section 65 should be tightened to indicate more clearly the essential purpose of a restriction order, that is, to protect the public from serious harm.

## Removal of the power to make a restriction order of limited duration; and Introduction of annual reports

5.16    These two recommendations are related. Section 65 enables a restriction order to be imposed with or without a time limit. The Butler Committee noted that it is a widely held view that a restriction order without a time limit is preferable to an order whose duration is prescribed, and they referred in this connection to *Gardiner's* case in which the then Lord Chief Justice (Lord Parker) said

> ". . . since in most cases the prognosis cannot be certain, the safer course is to make any restriction order unlimited in point of time. The only exception is where the doctors are able to assert confidently that recovery will take place within a fixed period when the restriction order can properly be limited to that period."****

---

\*        Cmnd 6244. Para 14.24.
\*\*       *'A Human Condition'*. Vol 2 pp 75-79.
\*\*\*     Cmnd 169. Para 519.
\*\*\*\*   Cmnd 6244. Para 14.25. R v Gardiner 1967 (1 WLR 464).

The Butler Committee also referred to the report of the Aarvold Committee* which had stressed the value of making restriction orders without limit of time. Many of those giving evidence before the Butler Committee on this point were of the opinion that all restriction orders should be made without limit of time. The Committee considered that the argument that it is generally not possible at the time of making of the order to determine how long it will be before the patient recovers was a strong one, and they recommended that the facility for making a limited restriction order should be removed from the section. However, as a safeguard against abuse, since a power to detain for an unlimited period carries with it the danger that detention may be maintained longer than is strictly necessary, they proposed that regular reports on patients under restriction orders should be made by the treating doctor to the Home Office.

5.17   The Consultative Document's recommendation was generally supported in the comments received, although there was some dissent notably from BASW and MIND. BASW** took the view that it was a major objection to section 65, involving serious injustice, that under it an offender could be detained for longer than would have been the case were he subject to normal penal sanctions. They suggested that, if it was thought that an offender presented a danger to the public which made it desirable for him to be detained for a longer period than the sentence a court would have imposed, the civil procedures for detention under section 26 should be invoked, so that the patient has available to him the full range of safeguards provided for such patients. In support of their suggestion, BASW pointed out that offenders who were not mentally disordered could not in general be sent to prison for indeterminate periods and had to be released from prison after fixed terms despite the fact that, according to the statistical evidence, they were quite likely to be reconvicted.

5.18   MIND*** took a similar line and suggested that the Butler recommendations were inadequate because they failed to address the underlying problem, which is that any indeterminate power creates the danger that the detention may be longer than is strictly necessary. MIND acknowledged that, by the nature of his office, the Home Secretary must observe strict standards for the protection of the public, and they accepted that regular reports from the Responsible Medical Officer might help him carry out his functions; but they did not consider that the adoption of the recommendation for annual reports from the Responsible Medical Officer on restricted patients could be regarded as an adequate safeguard of the patients' liberty. Although an undertaking had been given to Parliament during the passage of the 1959 Act to arrange for regular reports on restricted patients, MIND were aware of a number of cases where restricted patients had been detained for what MIND considered to be inordinately long periods.

5.19   In MIND's view, when a mentally disordered person has been convicted of a criminal offence, society is justified in protecting itself by holding him in custody for a period proportional to the gravity of his offence.

---

*   Cmnd 5191. '*Report on the Review of Procedures for the Discharge and Supervision of Psychiatric Patients Subject to Special Restrictions*'. HMSO (1973).

**  '*Mental Health Crisis Services—a New Philosophy*'. Para 40.

*** '*A Human Condition*'. Vol 2. pp 91 to 95.

During that period, society should do all that it can to rehabilitate him by offering treatment in a psychiatric hospital, whenever possible on a voluntary basis. Society should not, however, make use of a compulsory measure like the restriction order by seeking to disguise it as a treatment measure. In their view, the purpose of a restriction order should be recognised as being purely custodial, that is entirely for the protection of the public rather than for the benefit of the patient. MIND pointed out that some psychiatrists have argued that restriction orders are anti-therapeutic because they tie the responsible doctor's hands in preventing him from being able to grant leave or arrange for transfer or discharge of his patient without the Home Secretary's consent. They believe it wrong that all mentally disordered offenders should be treated differently in this respect from other offenders simply because they have been diagnosed as mentally disordered, particularly when the evidence does not justify such a distinction. According to MIND, the evidence suggests that the best indicators of future dangerous behaviour appear to be not the offender's mental abnormality, if any, but the number of previous convictions he has and the type and severity of the offence in question.

5.20    In the light of these considerations, MIND* put forward the following proposals—

'(1)    Restriction orders of unlimited duration

The trial judge should be authorised (but not compelled) to make an unlimited restriction order only if the defendant is convicted of clearly specified offences which involve serious violence against person or property....

(2)    Restriction orders of limited duration

The trial judge should be authorised to make a restriction order of limited duration for any imprisonable offence. It would be made for a maximum period (decided in each case by the trial judge), but no minimum would be named. The trial judge, in determining the length of the restriction order, should apply the same principles used for ordinary offenders—for example, the length of the sentence should be proportional to the gravity of the offence.

(3)    Therapeutic detention

After a restriction order has expired, treatment should be available on a voluntary basis. If the offender refuses to accept informal confinement to receive treatment, and is still unfit to be released, he could be detained only through civil procedures with appropriate safeguards.'

Alternatively, section 60/65 patients could be detained on a similar basis to prisoners transferred to hospital under sections 72 and 74 of the Act (whose position is discussed in paragraphs 5.41 to 5.51, below).

5.21    The provisions for the making of restriction orders are based on the recommendations of the Royal Commission**. In making the relevant proposals, the Royal Commission explicitly said that they considered it legitimate for society to protect itself from certain dangerous, mentally disordered offenders by detaining them in hospital for longer than would

* *Ibid.* pp 96-7.
** Cmnd 169. Paras 518, 519 and 526.

49

be justified by the gravity of their offence. The Commission did not make very clear what considerations they thought should guide the courts in determining the length of time for which special restrictions should be imposed in particular cases, although in accepting the concept of the restriction order of limited duration the Royal Commission clearly envisaged that in some cases it is possible to predict when an offender will cease to be dangerous. The Butler Committee appear to have adopted a similar view, except that in recommending removal of the power to make a restriction order of limited duration, they were less sanguine than the Commission about the reliability of such predictions. In Volume 2 of *'A Human Condition'*, however, MIND bring the Commission's central premise into question. As explained above, they argue that mentally abnormal offenders are apparently no more dangerous than other offenders, and hence that the law should be amended so as to ensure that in determining the length of restriction orders the courts should apply the same principles as are used for ordinary offenders. They produce statistics which purport to show that restricted patients are detained for substantially longer periods than prisoners who have committed comparable offences.

5.22    The primary object of a restriction order is to guard against the discharge of an offender from hospital by the health authorities while there remains a real risk of further and serious crime. This—and not the question whether the period of detention reflects the gravity of the offence—is the consideration which weighs with the Home Secretary in exercising his responsibility for restricted patients. As a result the period of detention may be much shorter than the appropriate term of imprisonment would have been. But, as MIND claims, some restricted patients, particularly in the Special Hospitals, are, for the protection of the public, detained for longer periods than prisoners convicted of comparable offences.

5.23    What evidence there is does indeed suggest that the generality of mentally abnormal offenders are no more dangerous than other offenders convicted of similar offences. In the present context, however, the Government's concern is not with the dangerousness of mentally abnormal offenders generally, but with that of a small sub-group of them who are made subject to a restriction order because they are identified by the courts as presenting a special risk to the public. The evidence which MIND cites includes a study done by the Home Office Statistical Department which showed a lower reconviction rate in respect of 344 offenders discharged from mental hospitals in 1971 than that of 2,796 prisoners sentenced to 18 months' imprisonment or less who were also discharged in that year. But none of the ex-patients was, in fact, subject to restrictions at the time of discharge (though a small number of them had been at an earlier stage). It is true that a separate study carried out by the Home Office Research Unit for the Aarvold Committee* showed that the rate of reconviction of male restricted patients conditionally discharged in 1966 and 1967 was substantially lower than that of prisoners released after serving sentences of 18 months. But that study does not justify the conclusion that the duration of the restrictions should have been limited to the appropriate sentence

---

* Cmnd 5191. Appendix 2.

50

of imprisonment for the offence. It is just as persuasive to argue that the study demonstrates that great care is taken in selecting the right time for discharge and in actively supervising the patients in the community.

5.24 Similar considerations arise in relation to the available evidence that mental disorder is of much less significance as a predictor of future dangerous behaviour than an offender's criminal history and the type and severity of his current offence. Here again, the Government believes that the matter must be judged, not in a general context, but in relation to a small number of mentally disordered offenders thought by the courts to present a special risk. Home Office experience in dealing with restricted patients (particularly those suffering from mental illness) over a number of years is that there is often a very strong causal connection between an offender's mental disorder and his capacity to do serious harm. For example, there are cases where delusions or hallucinations have prompted a mentally ill person to commit an offence and may powerfully dispose him towards the commission of further and serious crime. There are some cases where the causal link is more tenuous but it is rarely possible to feel confident that no such relationship exists. The contention that the duration of special restrictions should be related to the maximum or the actual term of imprisonment that might have been imposed for the offence is, therefore, in the Government's view, misconceived. It is normally impossible to forecast with any precision when the patient will no longer present any significant risk to others, and with dangerous offenders of this kind a restriction order of indefinite duration is usually appropriate. Such a restriction order ensures that when the patient's mental condition has improved to a point where the risk to the public has sufficiently receded the Home Secretary may authorise his discharge subject to conditions of residence and supervision. This procedure may enable a patient to be released earlier than would safely be possible if no conditions could be attached to his release.

5.25 In the light of these considerations the Government has come to the conclusion that the balance of advantage lies in leaving the law as it stands. The proposals put forward by MIND would, it is true, still maintain strong safeguards for the public because an unlimited period of restrictions would continue to be available where the offender committed a violent offence for which the maximum sentence is life imprisonment, and where such an offence has been committed in the past even though the current offence was less serious. But in the Government's view the proposals would significantly and unacceptably reduce the existing protection against the mentally disordered offender whom the court considers much more dangerous than is implicit in the particular offence for which he has been brought to trial. It is by no means unknown for offenders who, perhaps fortuitously, have never been convicted of any very grave offence, but who are nevertheless recognised as dangerous, to be accepted into the Special Hospitals; and the value of the indefinite restriction order in cases of this kind is well established. If there were to be introduced into the law a requirement that except in cases of serious violence, restriction orders should be of a finite duration proportional to the gravity of the offence, courts would have to relate the length of a restriction order simply and solely to the term of imprisonment that they would consider appropriate for the offence in question, had it been committed by a person falling outside the ambit of the Mental Health Act. If that happened, however, some mentally disordered offenders might well pass from the Home Secretary's control while they were still dangerous and while there was still a need to retain special safeguards against premature discharge.

5.26 BASW make the point that it is discriminatory to permit the indefinite detention of mentally disordered offenders in hospital, when there is no corresponding provision for the preventive detention of dangerous offenders who are either not mentally disordered or who, if they are, have not been made subject to a hospital order. The Government appreciates that the present law does not permit the indefinite detention in prison of dangerous offenders who have committed offences not carrying a life sentence. It does not, however, regard that as a good argument for abandoning the power that the existing law provides for the indeterminate detention of dangerous offenders who unquestionably fall within the ambit of the Mental Health Act. In the Government's view the law should continue to enable society to protect itself from certain dangerous mentally disordered offenders by detaining them in hospital for a period longer than would be justified by the gravity of their offence.

5.27 It remains to consider whether the Butler Committee's recommendation 109 on the removal of the power to make a restriction order of limited duration (see paragraph 5.16 above) should also be accepted. The Committee based this recommendation on the proposition, derived from the judgment in *Gardiner's* case, that since it is not generally possible at the time of making a restriction order to determine how long it will be before the patient recovers from his mental disorder, the only safe course is to make any restriction order unlimited in point of time. The *Gardiner* judgment, however, seems to be faulty in attempting to equate complete recovery from mental disorder with duration of dangerousness. An offender may cease to be dangerous and yet continue to suffer from some degree of mental disorder; indeed, many mentally disordered offenders will never be entirely free from mental disorder.

5.28 A more satisfactory formulation of the argument in favour of abolishing the court's power to make a finite restriction order might be to say that this course is justified because in practice it is impossible for courts to predict when an offender will cease to be dangerous. But even such a proposition rather overstates the matter. In certain cases where there is a good ground for expectation that an offender will soon recover from the disorder that has prompted his offence (for example, in cases of endogenous depression) it may be possible for the court, in the light of medical evidence, to make a reasonable prediction of when an offender will cease to be dangerous.

5.29 The Government considers, therefore, that the power to make a finite restriction order should not be removed from the statute book and that Butler recommendation 109 should be rejected. If recommendation 109 were rejected, it would not necessarily follow that recommendation 114 (relating to the provision of annual reports to the Home Secretary on the cases of all restricted patients) should also be rejected. In principle there is a good case for the provision of such reports as a safeguard against restricted patients being detained for unjustifiably long periods. As MIND pointed out, there are already extra-statutory arrangements for the provision of annual reports on the cases of restricted patients, following an undertaking which was given to Parliament during the passage of the 1959 Act. MIND suggest that these have not proved a very effective safeguard. The Government believes, however, that they are still potentially the most satisfactory form of safeguard and that their effectiveness could be enhanced if they were given statutory backing and if provision were made requiring the patient's Responsible Medical Officer to carry out an examination of him before submitting the report. The Government realises that the examination of patients and the writing of reports annually would impose some extra work on the doctors concerned, particularly on Special Hospital consultants. But it believes that Responsible Medical Officers will, as part of their general duties, be keeping their patients under regular observation and that they should be able to cope with this extra work. It is therefore proposed that the Butler recommendation for the provision of annual reports on restricted patients should be adopted.

### The consent of the receiving doctor

5.30 Under the present law, the decision to make a restriction order is a purely judicial one, and the court is under no duty, statutory or otherwise, to seek the view of the receiving consultant as to whether he is willing for the patient to be made subject to restriction. Section 65 provides that a restriction order cannot be made unless one of the doctors whose recommendations have been taken into account by the court has given evidence orally before the court. In practice, it is usually the prison medical officer who gives such oral evidence. Prison medical officers are occasionally asked by courts for their views on whether restrictions should be imposed; their present instructions make it clear that when they make a report to a court in support of a hospital order, they should not go on to recommend the imposition of restrictions. But if the prison doctor is the only medically qualified person in court when the question of disposal is under consideration, and he is asked to expand orally on his report and to assist the court in deciding on restrictions, he may find it very difficult to avoid expressing a view. Difficulties have occasionally arisen where a prison doctor has advised a court that, in his view, a restriction order is justified in a particular case, but the receiving consultant has subsequently objected to treating the patient under such restrictions.

5.31 The Butler Committee* took note of a strong feeling amongst many in the medical profession that courts should not be able to impose restriction orders without the consent of the receiving consultant. In its report, the Committee referred to cases which had occasionally occurred in which a hospital doctor had recommended a hospital order and had expressed his willingness to receive the patient, only to find that a restriction order had been added; in some of these cases, had the doctor been consulted about this, he would have made it clear that he was unwilling to accept the patient under such restrictions. Whilst deprecating any refusal ever, as a matter

* Cmnd 6244. Paras 14.22 and 14.23.

of principle, to receive a restricted patient, the Committee recognised that there might be reasonable grounds for refusal of particular cases on particular occasions. The Committee had no doubt that as a matter of good practice courts should invariably consult the receiving doctor before making a restriction order, and it accordingly recommended that the doctor's consent to accept the patient under restrictions should be required. The Committee argued that consultants would be likely to recommend hospital orders in more cases than they do at present, if the risk of a restriction order being imposed without their agreement were removed. On the other hand, it was hoped that consultants would be careful to use their right of refusal only in really justifiable cases.

5.32 The Consultative Document,* whilst recognising that restriction orders make some consultants feel unduly constrained in treating their patients and not free to make their own decisions in the crucial areas of discharge, transfer and leave, took the view that courts must be able to make such arrangements as they consider necessary for the protection of the public in relation to dangerous offenders. The Document went on to suggest that some doctors do not understand the effect and purpose of restriction orders and that much could be done to increase the co-operation of receiving doctors by consulting them beforehand about suggestions that restriction orders should be imposed. It was not suggested that this should be a statutory requirement, but rather that there was scope for administrative action to encourage such co-operation. It is clear from the comments that this is another area in which strong views are held, and opinion was fairly evenly divided.

5.33 The Government accepts the Butler Committee's view that there may well be proper reasons why a doctor feels he is able to offer treatment to a patient under a section 60 order, but unable to do so if a section 65 order is added. It is also concerned about the signs of increasing reluctance on the part of both doctors and other staff to accept offender patients for treatment, in particular those under restriction orders. This reluctance is likely to be exacerbated rather than improved if courts continue to be able to impose restriction orders against the wishes of the receiving hospital. On the other hand, although the Butler Committee hoped that consultants would not use any right of refusal of restricted patients indiscriminately, the Government is concerned about the likely consequences of making the consultant's agreement a prior condition to the making of a restriction order. The Government would wish to avoid placing the courts in a situation where, because of the objections of staff at a particular hospital, they were unable to impose restrictions on an offender whom they considered to be a serious danger to the public but who was clearly in need of hospital treatment.

5.34 In this sensitive area, it seems especially important to work towards co-operation and consensus rather than risk a worsening of relations between hospital staff and the courts. The Government believes that this can best be done by new arrangements designed to make receiving hospitals aware of the possibility that, in cases where the offence is serious enough

---

* Para 10.21.

to warrant this, the court might wish to add a restriction order, and to give them the opportunity to express a view on any difficulties which the imposition of such an order would create before the court makes its decision. If such difficulties are brought to their attention it would then be for the court to decide whether it would be right to make a hospital order with restrictions in the particular case. Where a hospital felt that the addition of a restriction order would present such problems that it would be unable to accept the patient, it would so inform the court, giving reasons for this. The court would then decide whether to make the section 60 order without restrictions or to deal with the offender in another way—eg by sending him to prison. The new arrangements proposed would involve a combination of legislative amendment and guidance to both courts and health authorities.

### Admission of conditionally discharged restricted patients by order of the Home Secretary to a 'place of safety'

5.35  A restricted patient who has been conditionally discharged is liable to be recalled to hospital by the Home Secretary at any time if his behaviour gives cause for anxiety. In practice it is usual for the Home Secretary to seek the agreement of the hospital to a patient's readmission and occasionally, because of the consultant's reluctance to take the patient back, this cannot be arranged at once. The Butler Committee* felt that this delay could place the supervising officer in a difficult position. The Committee therefore recommended that it should be possible for the Home Secretary to order the patient's detention in a 'place of safety' (which, pending the establishment of regional secure psychiatric units, might be the hospital of a local remand prison or remand centre) for up to 72 hours. The idea was to give the supervising officer the opportunity to take a conditionally discharged restricted patient out of the community for a limited period during which hospital staff might be persuaded to accept him as an in-patient.

5.36  In the Consultative Document** it was suggested that it was unrealistic to assume that the Responsible Medical Officer who knew the circumstances of a discharged restricted patient who had been under his care would change his mind about the desirability of recall within such a short period as 72 hours. It was also thought arguable whether it was right to use a penal institution even for a short period as a 'place of safety' when the patient had not committed any new offence.

5.37  There was little comment on this issue in the response to the Consultative Document. What little there was provided no grounds for taking a different view from that set out in the Document. The Government does not therefore propose to accept this recommendation. However, in guidance to be issued following amending legislation, supervising officers and hospital staff will be encouraged to maintain close contact with each other and try to agree on a practicable solution whenever problems arise with conditionally discharged restricted patients.

---

\* Cmnd 6244. Para 14.31.
\*\* Para 10.24.

## The Transfer of Prisoners to Hospital
### Sentenced prisoners

5.38 Section 72 of the Act provides power for the Home Secretary to direct that a person serving a sentence of imprisonment or other detention should be removed to and detained in a specified hospital. Before making such a direction the Home Secretary must be satisfied by reports from at least two medical practitioners (one of whom has been approved under section 28 of the Act) that the prisoner is suffering from mental illness, psychopathic disorder, subnormality or severe subnormality of a nature or degree warranting his detention in hospital for medical treatment. The Home Secretary must also be of the opinion that the transfer is expedient, having regard to the public interest and all the circumstances.

5.39 A transfer direction given in respect of a sentenced prisoner has the same effect as a hospital order. A restriction order may be added to it, if the Home Secretary thinks fit, by the use of section 74. If the transfer is made without restrictions, the person concerned ceases to be subject to his prison sentence and so may be discharged by his Responsible Medical Officer, the hospital managers or a Mental Health Review Tribunal. A prisoner who is transferred to hospital with restrictions under section 74 is, however, subject to the provisions of section 65 and thus cannot for the duration of his sentence be discharged, transferred to another hospital or given leave without the Home Secretary's consent. Whilst in hospital he remains subject to his prison sentence and may, if he no longer requires treatment, be sent back to prison. Alternatively, the Home Secretary may exercise any power of releasing him on licence or discharging him under supervision which could have been exercised if he had been remitted to prison. If he is still in hospital when the full term of his sentence expires the restrictions cease to have effect but he remains detained as if he had been admitted on that date in pursuance of a hospital order without restrictions. This means that there is legal authority for his further detention for one year. After that, the normal provisions of the Act for renewal of compulsory detention apply. A prisoner who is transferred to hospital subject to restrictions under section 74 is not entitled to request the Home Secretary to refer his case to a Tribunal for advice until a year after the transfer, just as a patient made the subject of a hospital order with restrictions under section 65 has to wait a year before requesting a Tribunal reference. The Home Secretary is under a duty to grant the request when made. A prisoner transferred without restrictions, like a patient made the subject of a hospital order without restrictions, can apply to a Tribunal within the period of 6 months from the date of transfer.

5.40 In the majority of cases, when a sentenced prisoner is transferred to hospital a restriction order is added. Thus, of 43 prisoners transferred to hospital under section 72 in 1976, only 6 were not subject to restrictions under section 74. There has been a marked decline in recent years in the use made of the power to transfer sentenced prisoners. In 1966, 149 sentenced prisoners were transferred to hospital, of whom 16 were not made subject to restrictions. In 1966, roughly three-quarters of the prisoners transferred subject to restrictions went to local hospitals, and the remainder to Special Hospitals. The proportion going to local hospitals has declined since then and was roughly two-thirds in 1976. The Butler Committee and MIND have both made a number of proposals for changes in sections 72 and 74. These are discussed below.

*The scope of section 72*

5.41   The Butler Committee* recommended that the scope of section 72 should be widened so that transfer to hospital could be made if the prisoner concerned was suffering from 'any form of mental disorder' and not just one of the four types of disorder specified in section 4 of the Act. The Committee had two objects in mind. The first was to avoid any reference in section 72 to the dubious concept of 'psychopathic disorder' (which they wished to see replaced by the term 'personality disorder'). The other was to allow the transfer, with his consent, of a prisoner suffering from, for example, sexual deviancy, drug addiction or alcoholism if suitable facilities were offered to him in a NHS hospital for the treatment or moderation of his condition.

5.42   The proposals made in Chapter 1, to exclude drug or alcohol dependence and sexual deviancy in themselves from the scope of the Act and to retain the term 'psychopathic disorder', make it unnecessary to pursue this recommendation further.

*Rights of prisoners transferred subject to restriction orders*

5.43   The Home Secretary's current practice is almost invariably to impose restrictions on transfer of a prisoner under section 72, the only exceptions being prisoners transferred a month or less before their earliest date of release (EDR) from prison (though in exceptional cases some of these are also transferred with restrictions). The reasons for this are—

  i. to preserve the right to send a patient back to prison if his condition improves significantly or is found not to be treatable or not to require treatment;

  ii. to ensure that, generally speaking, a transferred prisoner is not set at liberty substantially earlier than he would have been if he had remained in prison or Borstal;

  iii. to enable arrangements for compulsory supervision of a patient to be made as a condition of his discharge where this takes place before the expiration of the original sentence.

5.44   Some doubts were expressed to the Butler Committee** about the propriety of transferring a prisoner to hospital at a relatively late stage in his sentence; it was suggested that this practice was tantamount to imposing a second sentence. The Butler Committee, whilst understanding such anxieties, thought they were almost entirely theoretical because of the safeguards which exist against improper detention in hospital (eg the fact that transfer can only be effected on the basis of two medical reports and that in practice the consent of the receiving hospital has to be obtained). Moreover, even where restrictions have been imposed, they expire with the

---

\* Cmnd 6244. Para 3.45.
\*\* *Ibid.* Paras. 3.41 to 44.

original sentence and a patient's discharge then becomes entirely a matter for the Responsible Medical Officer. The Committee went on to consider whether, on expiration of the sentence, detention in hospital should require fresh admission procedures under Part IV of the Act, but they decided not to recommend this because they believed that a transferred patient, like any other compulsorily detained patient, would be discharged as soon as he was fit. However, in order to provide additional reassurance on this point, the Committee recommended:

    i. that every prisoner transferred under section 72 should have the right of application to a Tribunal when what would have been his EDR is reached; and

    ii. that when restrictions under section 74 have been added, the Home Secretary should review, at what would have been the EDR of the patient concerned, the need for them to continue and should remove them if possible.

5.45    MIND* take a different view. They argue that the guiding principle of the law relating to mentally disordered offenders should be that once an offender has been detained for a period proportional to the gravity of his offence, he should not be detained further except under Part IV powers. MIND did not share the Butler Committee's confidence in the adequacy of the present arrangements and drew attention to the following respects in which they considered the position of a section 72/74 patient to be unsatisfactory:

    i. Restrictions do not lapse until the full term of the sentence has expired so that the patient loses any benefit of remission of sentence which he would normally have earned—this can be up to a third of the original sentence.

    ii. The criteria for transferring a patient to hospital under section 72 are less stringent than those for admission under section 26. A section 26 admission can be made only if 'necessary in the interests of the patient's health or safety or for the protection of other persons', whereas the Home Secretary, in authorising a transfer, must merely be 'of opinion having regard to the public interest and all the circumstances that it is expedient'. Also, an adult suffering from subnormality or psychopathic disorder cannot at present be compulsorily admitted to hospital under section 26 whereas, if he is serving a prison sentence, he can be transferred to hospital under section 72 and may have to remain there after the expiry of his sentence.

    iii. Once in hospital, the rights of a transferred prisoner are marginally less than those of a section 26 patient, ie the nearest relative does not have a power of discharge.

    iv. A transferred prisoner is detained in hospital as the result of his offence and so is in the same position as a hospital order patient, ie, he is stigmatised as both an offender and somebody who is mentally disordered.

* '*A Human Condition*'. Vol 2 Chapter 6.

v. Most transferred prisoners in practice go to the Special Hospitals where, according to MIND, 'sheer administrative inertia' makes it likely that they will remain after their sentence has expired.* MIND also argue that placement in a Special Hospital is an infringement of liberty if such a degree of security is not necessary.

5.46 To remedy these alleged shortcomings, MIND suggested that—

i. A transferred prisoner should no longer be liable to detention under section 72 after what would have been his EDR, and if there is then a need for compulsory detention this should be met by making an application under section 26.

ii. A transferred prisoner should have the right to apply to a Tribunal on what would have been his EDR.

iii. A Mental Health Review Tribunal should have power to recommend transfer from a Special to a local hospital.

5.47 As the law stands at present, a patient who is subject to a transfer direction under section 72 accompanied by a direction restricting discharge under section 74 remains subject to the restrictions until the expiration of his sentence. This is defined as the expiration of the period during which he would have been liable to be detained in prison if the transfer direction had not been given. There is no legal right to remission of sentence, and it follows that any references to the period during which a prisoner is liable to be detained are references to the period of the full sentence as passed by the court. The Butler Committee assumed, in making recommendation 131, that this would continue to be the law. MIND's first proposal would, however, involve amending the Mental Health Act to provide that the restriction direction should cease to have effect on the date on which the patient could have been discharged from prison on remission of part of his sentence under the prison rules (the EDR). In the Government's view there are sound arguments for such an amendment. It does seem wrong that somebody who becomes mentally disordered after his release from prison is liable to detention only under civil powers whereas a person who, perhaps quite fortuitously, becomes mentally disordered while in prison can be transferred to hospital and detained there subject to restrictions even after the date when he would normally have been released from prison.

5.48 It was pointed out in paragraph 5.43, above, that one of the main reasons for imposing restrictions under section 74 is to ensure that, generally speaking, a transferred prisoner is not set at liberty substantially earlier than he would have been if he had remained in prison or Borstal. (In this respect, the object of a restriction order imposed under section 74 can be said to be different from that of one imposed under section 65, where the primary object is to safeguard the public against the risk of a dangerous offender being prematurely discharged by his doctor). This does not require the continuance of restrictions after what would have been EDR has been reached.

5.49 It is certainly true that there is a small number of cases in which a mentally disordered offender who has been transferred to hospital under section 72 is clearly dangerous and there would be some advantage in being

---

* Most transfers are in fact to local hospitals and not to the Special Hospitals.

able to ensure his continued detention at least until his latest date of release has been reached. Clearly, however, the sentence imposed would have to be one of some duration for this advantage to be of practical significance. Unless there had been some marked deterioration in the prisoner's mental condition, it would be hard to justify the general principle of maintenance of control for the duration of the full sentence by reference to such cases, without appearing to imply that the court may have under-estimated the risk that the offender presents. The protection that the present law affords is at best partial since regardless of the patient's dangerousness any restrictions must still cease to have effect on the expiration of the full term of the sentence. In any case, procedures for detention under Part IV of the Act are also concerned with protection of the public from possibly dangerous patients, and these could be invoked where there had been a deterioration in the mental condition of a transferred patient which made him likely to be a danger to others. Moreover, whilst protection of the public might be regarded as a good argument for maintaining restrictions beyond EDR in a small number of cases where the offender patient was clearly dangerous, it can certainly not be regarded as a convincing argument for maintaining restrictions in all cases. Under the Scottish Mental Health Act, restrictions cease to apply on what what would have been the prisoner's EDR, and no particular difficulties appear to have been encountered there. The Government, therefore, proposes that restrictions under section 74 should cease to apply on what would have been the EDR of a prisoner transferred under section 72. If the law were changed in this way it would be unnecessary to pursue further the Butler Committee's recommendation that the Home Secretary should review the need to continue restrictions at EDR.

5.50   The Government thinks there is substance in MIND's point that the nearest relative has no power to discharge a transferred prisoner. It does seem wrong that a person who, perhaps fortuitously, becomes mentally ill while serving a prison sentence should be treated less advantageously after the date of what would have been his EDR has passed, than a person admitted to hospital under the normal compulsory procedures. It is therefore proposed that transferred prisoners who continue to be detained after EDR should be detained as if under section 26.

5.51   The simplest way of achieving this result may be by an amendment of the law providing that a sentenced prisoner transferred to hospital under section 72 should be treated at what would have been his EDR as if he had been admitted to hospital on that date on an application under section 26, with the usual procedures for the making of such an order being waived. It does not seem necessary, particularly in cases where the prisoner has been transferred shortly before his EDR, to go through the process of actually making a section 26 application since this would involve much the same considerations as were involved in making the transfer itself. Nor does there seem to be a need to introduce a 'treatability' requirement, because a prisoner would only have been transferred under section 72 in the first place if he appeared likely to benefit from treatment. If no benefit were gained the opportunity would already have been taken (assuming the prisoner had been transferred subject to restrictions) to send him back to prison. The usual criteria, would apply on renewal. The effect of this would be that the Responsible Medical Officer, the hospital managers and the nearest relative (subject to barring procedures) would have power to discharge the patient immediately after what would have been his EDR; and, if none of them did so, the patient would be able to apply to a Tribunal. If the Tribunal failed to discharge the patient, the order would then remain in force for 6 months (under the Government's proposal for halving the periods of detention for section 26 patients), unless it were renewed for a further period.

### Other Prisoners

5.52   Under section 73 of the Act, the Home Secretary may authorise the removal from prison to hospital of certain categories of unsentenced prisoners. The main categories are prisoners who have been committed in custody for trial or sentence at the Crown Court, but the section also applies to persons remanded in custody by a magistrates' court and civil prisoners*. The conditions which have to be satisfied before such a transfer can be made are the same as those for a transfer under section 72, except that the power is limited to persons suffering from mental illness or severe subnormality. Where the transfer direction is given in respect of an untried or unsentenced prisoner the Home Secretary is required by section 74(1) to impose restrictions on discharge. In 1976, 13 persons were transferred to hospital under section 73.

5.53   Section 73 was not discussed either in the Butler Report or in the Consultative Document. In Chapter 1 of Volume 2 of 'A Human Condition', MIND make a number of criticisms of the procedure for removal to hospital of persons committed for trial and call for changes in the law. Comments have also been received from the National Association for the Care and Resettlement of Offenders (NACRO).

5.54   MIND's main criticisms are that a restriction order can be imposed by the Home Secretary under sections 73/4 of the Act with relatively few safeguards. No determination need be made by a court that the defendant committed the offence with which he is charged, yet he may spend a long time in hospital because the doctors and the Home Secretary must act on the assumption that he actually performed the criminal act in question. The only requirement is that the Home Secretary be satisfied on the basis of two medical opinions that 'it is expedient' to make such an order. No social worker is involved; the nearest relative has no right of discharge and there is no right of appeal to a Mental Health Review Tribunal.

5.55   MIND and NACRO both feel that it is improper to subject a person to a restriction order if no court of law has determined that he has committed an imprisonable offence; they have put forward similar proposals. MIND** propose that—

---

* Section 73(2)(f) also refers to 'aliens detained . . . in pursuance of the Aliens Order 1953, or any order amending or replacing that Order', but since the 1953 Order has been replaced not by another order, but by the Immigration Act, 1971, the reference is now inoperative. The Government will introduce a suitable amendment reviving the power and extending it to all persons detained in pursuance of the 1971 Act.

** 'A Human Condition'. Vol 2 p 20.

"... when the time comes for the accused to stand trial (and this should not be postponed solely because of his disability, as seems to occur under section 73), the transfer direction should cease to have effect. After that, if the person is mentally competent, he should stand trial for the offence with which he is charged; and if he is convicted, the court has the option of making a hospital order, with or without restrictions, in accordance with the provisions of sections 60/65 of the Mental Health Act. If, on the other hand, the defendant is acquitted, the court has no jurisdiction over him, but he could then be civilly admitted to hospital if in need of treatment . . . . The question of whether the defendant is under disability may arise, so that the trial cannot proceed. In this event, the issue of disability should be determined in accordance with the Criminal Procedure (Insanity) Act 1964 . . ."

NACRO have, however, suggested that a few months might be allowed to elapse before such a hearing to allow for the possibility of a patient regaining capability.

5.56 The two aspects of the present law about which MIND and NACRO are concerned are: firstly, that it enables persons who are thought unfit to appear in the Crown Court to stand trial to be kept in the hospital to which they have been transferred for long periods of time, subject to the serious consequences of a restriction order, without any determination having been made by a court that they actually committed the offence; and secondly, that, in certain circumstances, the Crown Court may dispose of the case of a person who is unfit to appear in court by making a hospital order, with or without restrictions, in his absence and without having arrived at any findings of fact as to whether he actually committed the offence. The power in question is contained in section 76(2)(b) and (3) of the 1959 Act. Under these provisions, where an accused person who is awaiting trial in the Crown Court has been transferred to hospital and it appears to the Crown Court that it is impracticable or inappropriate to bring him to trial, the Court may make a hospital order, where necessary with restrictions, in the absence of the accused and without convicting him. The Court can do this if it is satisfied, on the evidence of two doctors, that the person is suffering from mental illness or severe subnormality of a nature or degree which warrants his detention in hospital for medical treatment. The Court must also be of opinion after considering any depositions or any other documents it may require, that it is proper to make a hospital order.

5.57 The Government accepts that there are unsatisfactory features of the present law with regard to persons who are unfit, by reason of their mental condition, to appear in the Crown Court to stand trial. These features were examined in detail in a consultative paper which the Home Office issued in April 1978 concerning the Butler Committee's recommendations (20-38) on disability in relation to trial generally. The remedies suggested in the paper were—

    i. that a limit of 6 months should be placed on the period of time for which the Crown Court may be allowed to postpone the trial of a person who is unfit to appear in court in the hope that his mental condition will improve; and

ii. that (on the assumption that a trial of the facts procedure, as recommended by the Butler Committee, is introduced for disability cases generally) provision should be made empowering the court to treat a person who is unfit to appear to stand trial as if he had been found under disability in relation to trial under the new procedure.

5.58 It remains to be seen whether these proposals will find approval from those whose views have been invited and, if so, how soon the Government would be able to introduce legislation giving effect to them. If the proposals are approved, the Goverment would wish to legislate on them as soon as possible. It seems clear, however, that any provisions for this purpose would have to form part of the legislation giving effect to the Butler Committee's recommendations on disability in relation to trial generally, and could not be introduced in isolation in advance of that legislation. Pending further legislation on this area of the law the Home Office will institute special arrangements for monitoring cases in which persons awaiting trial in the Crown Court are transferred to hospital under section 73, with a view to ensuring that the period of detention in hospital is kept to a minimum.

## REMANDS TO HOSPITAL AND INTERIM HOSPITAL ORDERS

5.59 The Butler Committee recommended* that courts should be given power to remand a mentally disordered person to hospital. They identified four situations in which this might be useful. These were—

i. where a medical report is required on a convicted defendant;
ii. where a defendant requires medical care during a custodial remand;
iii. where a period in hospital is required to determine whether a hospital order would be the most suitable disposal for a convicted offender;
iv. where a defendant is found under disability in relation to trial but the medical advice indicates the possibility of recovery within a few months, at least to the point at which he would be fit to stand trial.

5.60 The Committee proposed the creation of a new court order for all these situations which would be available equally at Special Hospitals or local psychiatric hospitals. The order would provide for the remand of a defendant to a particular hospital over a specified period of time. The order would last for a maximum of 3 months in the first two situations and for 3 months extendable to a maximum of 6 months in the last two. Remand to hospital was to be considered only if remand on bail was not feasible.

5.61 These proposals were welcomed in the Consultative Document** as being, in principle, a useful addition to the flexibility of criminal courts and their ability to dispose of each case in the most appropriate way. Reservations were, however, expressed as to whether all four situations could be covered by a single form of court order. It was also noted that certain

---

* Cmnd 6244. Paras 12.2 to 12.11.
** Paras 10.7 to 10.16.

of the proposals, for example those relating to medical reports and unfitness for trial, needed to be examined not only in the context of the review of the Mental Health Act but also in relation to criminal procedure generally.

5.62   Comments received on this part of the Consultative Document were generally favourable, although concern was expressed about the resource implications of the proposals and about the practicability of implementing them without the provision of sufficient secure accommodation.

5.63   In the light of this response, a consultation paper was issued in June, 1978 to all interested parties, including the judiciary, the magistracy, police and probation representative bodies and health and social services authorities. The paper reviews in turn each of the four situations in which the Butler Committee thought a power of remand to hospital would be valuable and, where appropriate, sets it in the context of criminal procedure generally. The paper concludes that the Mental Health Act should be amended to enable courts to remand defendants to hospital, as an alternative to a custodial remand, both where a psychiatric report is required and where the defendant requires treatment in hospital during a custodial remand. The maximum period of a remand to hospital for a psychiatric report would be 28 days rather than the 3 months suggested by the Butler Committee though the order might be extendable up to a maximum of 3 months. The power to remand for treatment would be confined to defendants suffering from mental illness or severe subnormality and would be available only in respect of offences punishable with imprisonment. The maximum period of the remand would be 3 months.

5.64   The paper also proposes that provision should be included in the legislation to amend the Mental Health Act enabling courts to make interim hospital orders. It suggests that these orders, the purpose of which would be to enable the court to be satisfied whether treatment in hospital was appropriate, should run initially for 3 months, but that they might be extendable up to 6 months.

5.65   As regards remands in cases of disability, the paper recognises that the Butler Committee's proposals would require separate legislation, the form of which cannot be determined until decisions have been taken on the Butler Committee's recommendations regarding disability in relation to trial generally.

5.66   The consultation paper also discusses the resource implications of the proposals for introducing remands to hospital for psychiatric report and/or treatment and interim hospital orders (paras. 41-46); the resource implications of the former are much greater than the latter (see para 9.5, below). The paper therefore proposes that the statutory provision for remands to hospital for psychiatric report and/or treatment would be made on the strict understanding that the relevant powers would not be brought into operation until the requisite manpower, financial and physical resources were available. The proposed provision for interim hospital orders would, however, be implemented at the first opportunity following legislation.

5.67   Comments on the paper have been requested by September 29th 1978. Any body or individual who has not received a copy of the paper but who would wish to do so should write to—

Room C521,
Department of Health and Social Security,
Alexander Fleming House,
Elephant and Castle,
LONDON, SE1 6BY.

SUMMARY OF PROPOSALS: CHAPTER 5

*Section 60*

i.   For patients suffering from psychopathic disorder or mental handicap there should be a requirement, both on admission to hospital and at renewal of detention, of likelihood of benefit from treatment (para 5.7)

ii.   present periods of detention under section 60 (both at admission and on renewal) should be halved (para 5.7).

iii.   medical recommendations made for the purposes of section 60 should not be made by two doctors from the same prison, hospital or other institution (para 5.7).

iv.   the provisions of section 28(4) of the Act should apply to medical recommendations made under Part V (para 5.7).

*Section 65*

i.   section 65 should be re-worded to indicate more clearly the essential purpose of a restriction order—that is, to protect the public from serious harm (para 5.15).

ii.   existing powers under section 65 to make restriction orders of indefinite duration should be retained (para 5.26).

iii.   the present power to make a restriction order of limited duration should be retained (para 5.29).

iv.   Responsible Medical Officers should be required by statute to make an annual report on each of their restricted patients (para 5.29).

v.   new arrangements should be introduced to make receiving hospitals aware, in cases where the offence is serious enough to warrant this, of the possibility that the court might wish to add a restriction order, and to give them the opportunity to express a view before the court makes its decision on any difficulties which the imposition of such an order would create. The new arrangements would involve a combination of legislative amendment and guidance to both courts and health authorities (para 5.34).

vi.   guidance should be issued following legislation to encourage hospital staff and supervising officers of restricted patients being recalled to hospital to maintain close contact (para 5.37).

*Sections 72 and 74*

i.   restrictions under section 74 should cease to apply on what would have been the earliest date of release of a prisoner transferred to hospital under section 72 (para. 5.49).

ii.  prisoners transferred to hospital under section 72 who are thought to require detention after what would have been their earliest date of release from prison should be treated as if admitted to hospital on that date under section 26, but with the usual procedures for the making a section 26 order being waived (para 5.51).

## Section 73

Proposals for changes to section 73 (set out in a consultative paper, '*Disability in Relation to Trial*') cannot be introduced in advance of legislation on disability in relation to trial generally: in the meantime, special arrangements will be instituted for monitoring the use of section 73 with a view to ensuring that the period of detention in hospital is kept to a minimum (para 5.58).

## Remands to hospital and interim hospital orders

Proposals for amendment to the Mental Health Act to allow courts to remand defendants to hospital and to allow them to make interim hospital orders have been set out in a consultative paper '*Remands to Hospital and Interim Hospital Orders*' (paras 5.63-5.67).

CHAPTER 6

# SAFEGUARDS FOR PATIENTS

## MENTAL HEALTH REVIEW TRIBUNALS

6.1 The Consultative Document* discussed a number of suggestions for change in the functions, powers and constitution of Mental Health Review Tribunals (MHRTs). It also announced that MHRT procedures were to be considered separately in an interdepartmental review under the aegis of the Lord Chancellor's Office in which the Council on Tribunals and the Chairmen of MHRTs would be invited to participate. A discussion paper on MHRT procedures is being issued by the Lord Chancellor's Office, and the outcome may be that some amendment to sections 123 and 124 of the Act will be necessary. This White Paper does not duplicate the ground covered in that review on procedures but concentrates instead on the functions, powers and constitution of Tribunals.

### Entitlement to Tribunal hearings

6.2 MHRTs have power under the Mental Health Act 1959 to discharge patients from detention in hospital or from guardianship. Patients over the age of 16 detained in hospital under sections 26 or 60 (provided the latter are not also subject to section 65 restrictions) and those placed under guardianship have a right to apply to a MHRT at any time within the first period of 6 months of detention or guardianship. They may also apply for a further review once within each renewed period of detention or guardianship. A patient detained under a section 60 order who is also subject to restrictions under section 65 cannot apply directly to a Tribunal but can ask the Home Secretary to refer his case to a Tribunal after his first year of detention: thereafter he may make further requests to the Home Secretary at the same intervals as those in which an unrestricted patient can apply direct to a Tribunal. The Home Secretary must refer the case to a Tribunal within two months of receiving the request, but is not bound by the Tribunal's recommendation. At present, orders for the detention of patients admitted to hospital under sections 26 or 60 (without restrictions) and guardianship orders run initially for one year and may then be renewed for a period of a further year and subsequently for two-yearly periods. Paragraphs 2.47 and 4.15, above, propose that these periods be halved to six months, followed by a further six months and periods of a year thereafter. This change will mean that patients will have twice as many opportunities to apply to a Tribunal as at present. A restricted patient would also have twice as many opportunities to request reference of his case, except that he cannot ask for this until the first year of detention has expired. He would already have had an opportunity to appeal against the court's decision to make a hospital order accompanied by a restriction order, and it is not proposed to reduce the initial period of one year before which

_____
* Paras 8.3 to 8.19.

a request for reference can be made. It is proposed that restricted patients should continue to have a right to request reference in their second year of detention but that the subsequent right should be increased to one a year instead of biennially.

*Automatic reviews*

6.3    Some patients lack the initiative to apply to a Tribunal and the Consultative Document* proposed that automatic reviews be instituted in addition to the increases proposed above. Comments indicate considerable support for automatic reviews though there is concern that too frequent reviews might become mere formalities. The Consultative Document suggested that automatic reviews should be at 'well-spaced intervals' and, bearing in mind the practicalities of Tribunal caseload, that a doubling of Tribunal cases would allow automatic reviews at the end of the first and fifth year of detention or at the end of the first six months and the fourth year of detention. For restricted patients, it suggested that the early review be omitted. Different views have been expressed about what would be appropriate intervals between automatic reviews, but there does seem to be general agreement that there should be an automatic review of unrestricted patients after six months and that an interval of four or five years between automatic reviews would be too long. The practicalities in terms of Tribunal caseload are an important factor and, though it seems clear that an increase would be welcomed by many Tribunal members, it has to be borne in mind that other suggestions made in this White Paper will also add considerably to the work of Tribunals. The Government therefore proposes that automatic reviews for patients who have not availed themselves of their right to apply within the normal intervals should be introduced for unrestricted patients after 6 months and thereafter at three-yearly intervals; and that, to allow for flexibility, provision should be made for the interval to be reduced by regulation in the light of experience. Automatic reviews at three-yearly intervals are also proposed for restricted patients who have not exercised their right, within the preceding three years, to request reference.

6.4    The effect of these proposed changes on the workload of Tribunals might be substantial, particularly in relation to existing restricted patients. They would also impose a heavy task on the staff of Special Hospitals because of the large number of restricted patients in these hospitals. There may also be a short term problem in the areas close to the Special Hospitals in obtaining the services of sufficient suitably qualified lawyers to act as Presidents of Tribunals and medical members with the right experience. In view of the considerable backlog of cases to be dealt with, automatic tribunal entitlement could not be introduced in full immediately after amending legislation; a delayed starting-date would be set for the implementation of this provision and interim arrangements made in respect of the backlog.

*Powers of Tribunals*

6.5    There has been general endorsement of the Consultative Document's** proposals for extending the powers of Tribunals to enable them to order delayed discharge (for up to three months) and to recommend

---

*    Paras 8.6 to 8.11.
** Paras 8.12 to 8.17.

trial leave, transfer to another hospital or conditional discharge. The distinction between ordering and recommending is an important one and takes account of the need for agreement of others, eg the receiving hospital or social services department. It is proposed to adopt the suggestion that a Tribunal should be informed if any of their recommendations are not accepted and why, and that, if not implemented within a specified time, the Tribunal should be able to make an alternative finding. Recommendations by Tribunals for trial leave and transfer to another hospital do not entail legislative change. The Act does not however make express provision for the conditional discharge of unrestricted patients from hospital. Section 39, under which a Responsible Medical Officer can authorise leave of absence, is in practice often used for this purpose, but the power to recall then only lasts for six months. The purpose of conditional discharge would generally be to ensure that on discharge the patient remained resident in a particular place or continued to undertake some specified form of treatment. These requirements could be met within any of the revised arrangements for compulsory powers in the community discussed in paragraphs 4.14 to 4.20, above, and if these are introduced it would be desirable also to give Tribunals power to recommend a patient's transfer to community care.

6.6    There has been general endorsement of the suggestion in the Consultative Document* that an application to a Tribunal should not be withdrawn without the Tribunal's permission and that, if withdrawn before being heard, it should not prevent a further application being made within the specified period. This proposal will therefore be adopted.

*Tribunal membership*

6.7    The Consultative Document** referred to MIND's*** recommendation that Tribunal membership be enlarged or altered to include a social worker. Comments have, for the most part, favoured this. In many cases social workers have a valuable role to play, particularly in advising on the range of alternatives available in the community or where trial leave is under consideration. There are arguments, however, against a rigid rule that Tribunals should always include a social worker. There may not always be a social worker available with the sort of mental health expertise required. Other professionals such as community psychiatric nurses might have an equally significant contribution to make. An insistence that a social worker be the third member would, moreover, exclude the truly 'lay' element on the Tribunal. On the other hand, to require that each Tribunal should be increased to four members would have implications both for the cost of Tribunal hearings and, of course, for social services departments' manpower. The Government believes that the best answer is for greater use to be made of the existing power to appoint a fourth Tribunal member, but not to make it a statutory requirement either that a social worker be appointed as fourth member or that a social worker should replace the third 'lay' member.

---

*       Para 8.18.
**     Para 8.19.
***   'A Human Condition'. Vol I, p 89.

6.8    There is general support for the more frequent involvement of forensic psychiatrists in Tribunal work. It has however to be recognised that
as yet there are very few forensic psychiatrists in the NHS.

*Restricted patients*

6.9    MIND* have proposed that Tribunals should no longer review restricted cases and that this role should be taken over by the Home Secretary's
Advisory Board on Restricted Patients which was set up following the report
of the Aarvold Committee.** MIND argued that whereas, in reviewing the
cases of unrestricted patients, Tribunals exercise a judicial function in determining whether a patient should continue to be detained, their function
in relation to restricted patients is clearly advisory. MIND questioned the
value of a review by Tribunals whose recommendations for discharge or
transfer were, they claimed, rejected almost as often as they are accepted,
whereas recommendations of the Advisory Board seemed generally to be
accepted by the Home Secretary.

6.10    The Aarvold Committee drew a distinction between the function
of the Advisory Board and that of a Tribunal. It said: 'the fundamental
purpose of the Tribunals is to act as a safeguard for the liberty of the
individual and to insure against unjustified detention in hospital, whereas
the body we have in mind would be looking critically at proposals for allowing individual patients greater liberty and considering whether they were
soundly based and acceptable on grounds of public safety.'*** It was to
avoid confusion between these functions that the Aarvold Report recommended the setting up of a separate board.

6.11    The Government thinks it right that the distinction in function
between the Advisory Board and Mental Health Review Tribunals should
be retained and that both bodies should continue to be concerned with
the cases of restricted patients. The main function of a Mental Health
Review Tribunal in considering such cases is to provide the Home Secretary
with advice, independent of that provided by the patient's Responsible
Medical Officer, on whether or not the patient's condition warrants further
detention in hospital, having regard to all relevant factors, one of which
would be any risk to the public if discharged. When the Home Secretary's
Advisory Board looks at a proposal for allowing a restricted patient greater
liberty the Board's only concern is to offer the Home Secretary advice
on whether the proposal is soundly based and acceptable having regard
to public safety. The aspect from which the Board approaches the matter
is thus much narrower and more specific than that of a Mental Health
Review Tribunal.

6.12    A patient under a section 65 restriction order who is discharged from
hospital before the order expires may be recalled to hospital by the Home
Secretary at any time. The Butler Committee**** suggested that in the

*      'A Human Condition'. Vol 2, pp. 174–5.
**     Cmnd 5191. 'Report on the Review of Procedures for the Discharge and Supervision of
       Psychiatric Patients Subject to Special Restrictions'. HMSO (1973).
***    Ibid. Para 35.
****   Cmnd 6244. Para 4.24.

case of former Special Hospital patients the Advisory Board should always be involved in considering whether recall is necessary. The Government does not support this but thinks that the recall of a restricted patient to hospital should be followed by reference to a Tribunal within a month of recall. It proposes that these arrangements should apply to patients from NHS hospitals as well as former Special Hospital patients.

6.13   It is proposed to make other changes to the Act as it relates to Mental Health Review Tribunals. Some of these are consequential on changes discussed elsewhere in this Paper, for example in the criteria for renewal of detention or guardianship, which will need to be reflected in the circumstances in which the patient should be discharged by a Tribunal. Further amendments will no doubt be needed in the light of proposals by the Committee on Mental Health Review Tribunal Procedures which has, in particular, suggested an extensive revision of the Tribunal Rules drawn up by the Lord Chancellor in accordance with section 124 of the Act.

### CONSENT TO TREATMENT: TREATMENT OF DETAINED PATIENTS

6.14   One of the most controversial issues with which this White Paper is concerned is whether, and if so to what extent, the law should authorise doctors and other staff to impose treatment on patients detained under the Mental Health Act. On the basis of the legal advice available to it, the Department of Health and Social Security has taken the view that, where the purpose of detention is treatment, the 1959 Act gives the Responsible Medical Officer implied authority to treat a patient in relation to his mental disorder, if necessary without the consent of the patient or any other person. Nevertheless, the Department has always advised doctors to obtain if possible the consent of both the patient and the nearest relative (although the latter consent has no validity in law) before beginning a form of treatment which involves any appreciable risk. The Medical Defence Union, on the basis of independent legal opinion, has given similar advice to its members in its booklet 'Consent to Treatment'. However, this view, which has never been tested in the courts, has recently been increasingly questioned. The Royal College of Psychiatrists, the Butler Committee, MIND and the Davies Committee have all called for clarification of the position; and in September 1977, in a booklet 'The Management of Violent or Potentially Violent Patients'*, the Confederation of Health Service Employees quoted the view of their legal adviser that the 1959 Act cannot be taken to confer on staff any right to impose treatment on detained patients without consent. The Government wishes to remove any uncertainty and proposes to amend the Act to define the extent to which treatment for mental disorder can be imposed.

6.15   As is emphasised in paragraph 1.6, above, there is no provision in the 1959 Act either authorising or implying that treatment can be imposed on an informal (ie voluntary) patient without his consent. No change in this position is contemplated, and no change in the Act is considered to be required in this respect.

---

* Para 72.3.

71

6.16  As regards detained patients, the Government's view is that the power to impose treatment in certain circumstances needs to be made specific rather than to be implied as at present and intends to make it clear that staff may, in certain circumstances, as well as in an emergency, need to impose treatment on a detained patient without his consent.

6.17  Any legislative provision on this matter must also of course provide adequate safeguards for patients. It would be unacceptable for example to allow the imposition of *all* forms of treatment—in particular those which are hazardous or irreversible—without a second opinion. It is by no means easy to formulate proposals which will provide both safeguards for patients and sufficient flexibility to enable staff to deal with the variety of difficult situations which confront them. Difficult and disruptive patients are the ones most likely to refuse consent to treatment needed to ameliorate their condition, and, if staff are to undertake more than a custodial role, it must be possible for essential treatment to be given. It will be important that any new arrangements concerning consent to treatment do not increase staff reluctance to undertake the care and treatment of potentially disruptive or difficult patients. The suggestions in the following paragraphs aim at an appropriate balance between these different interests.

*General principles*

6.18  The proposed treatment and its likely effects should be explained to the patient in terms which he is able to understand. His consent should always be sought; if he refuses and there are alternative methods of treatment available which he might find more acceptable, these should be offered. Where it is not possible to agree with the patient the form the treatment is to take and the consultant feels the imposition of treatment is essential he should, wherever there is a choice, select the method of treatment the patient finds least objectionable or which would represent the minimum interference with the patient. Special considerations apply where the patient is incapable of understanding the nature and effects of the treatment; these are discussed in paragraphs 6.23 to 6.25.

6.19  The Butler Committee suggested* that 'Treatment (other than nursing care) should not be imposed on any patient without his consent if he is able to appreciate what is involved' but went on to list three circumstances in which staff should be authorised to give treatment without consent. These are—

i. where (not being of a hazardous or irreversible character) it represents the minimum interference with the patient to prevent him from behaving violently or otherwise being a danger to himself or to others: *or*

ii. where it is necessary to save the patient's life: *or*

iii. where (not being irreversible) it is necessary to prevent him from deteriorating.

* Cmnd 6244. Paras 3.50–3.59.

The Committee also suggested that where, by reason of his disability, the patient is unable to appreciate what is involved, despite the help of an explanation in simple terms, it should be possible to impose treatment but that special considerations should apply to treatment involving irreversible procedures.

6.20   Although the Butler Committee was concerned only with offender patients the same arguments and principles are thought to apply to all detained patients. The Consultative Document* suggested that a formula based on these ideas would provide the right balance but that the special considerations involving irreversible procedures should be extended to cover controversial treatments or those not fully established in clinical practice. Comments on the Document indicate a good deal of support for these ideas. However, some thought the formula was too restrictive and some that it was too wide. Others argued that to deny a consultant the right to impose the treatment he believes is necessary could result in the illness being untreated and its course remaining unchecked. Some, on the other hand, suggested that allowing treatment to be imposed 'in order to prevent deterioration' was open to such a wide interpretation as to be meaningless.

6.21   The Government believes that an approach on the broad lines suggested by the Butler Committee is most likely to provide the right balance. It has the advantages that—

    i. it puts limitations on the power to impose treatment without consent;

    ii. it distinguishes between patients who can appreciate what is involved and those who cannot; and

    iii. it recognises the need for special arrangements for certain types of treatment, eg between hazardous, irreversible or not fully established treatment.

*Common law defence*

6.22   The Butler Committee commented that 'Certain eventualities, such as the need to restrain a patient during a violent episode by the injection of a tranquilliser, or to use medical procedures to save the life of a patient who lacks understanding, would be covered by common law, treatment being justified on the ground of presumed consent or necessity'.** The common law does indeed provide cover in such situations by affording a defence of lawful justification and excuse in any legal proceedings which might follow. It is understood however that this common law defence only applies in emergencies where immediate action is necessary and where the treatment is for the purpose of bringing that emergency to an end. An 'emergency' is taken to mean circumstances in which *immediate* action is necessary to preserve the life of the patient or to prevent serious deterioration of his condition. It would include circumstances in which a patient became violent and was likely to be dangerous to himself or others, and treatment was imposed for the purpose of controlling him; but the doctor

---

*   Para 8.23.
** Cmnd 6244. Para 3.57.

or other staff concerned would have to justify its use as reasonable. The common law defence is thus rather limited, and the Government believes that it would be right to make it explicit that staff have authority to impose treatment on a detained patient where this is necessary to *prevent* an emergency from arising.

*Valid consent*

6.23    Valid consent implies the ability, given an explanation in simple terms, to understand the nature, purpose and effect of the proposed treatment. A patient may of course be able to understand the nature, purpose and effect of one treatment but not of another; and his capacity to understand may vary from time to time. Before giving treatment, it is accepted good professional practice to seek consent wherever the patient is capable of giving a valid consent. The Government's view is that if a detained patient who is capable of giving valid consent refuses to give it the doctor should not be able to impose any treament (except in emergency) without a concurring second opinion. There are certain treatments, referred to in paragraph 6.25 below, which in its view should not be imposed on a patient without his consent under any circumstances (again except in an emergency). If the patient is plainly not capable of giving a valid consent the Government considers that the consultant should be able to impose such treatment as he considers necessary to alleviate or cure the mental disorder (except the forms of treatment referred to in paragraph 6.25 below), but should first, where possible, consult a relative or friend who is close to the patient and take account of his views. Where the patient or others disagree that he is unable to give a valid consent, the doctor should seek a second opinion both on whether the patient has sufficient understanding to consent to, or refuse, treatment, and on whether any refusal should be overridden. The form of the second opinion is discussed in paragraphs 6.28 and 6.29, below.

*Treatment for conditions unrelated to the mental disorder*

6.24    The question arises as to whether treatments other than those relating to the patient's mental disorder should be included in these arrangements. The arguments for imposing treatment on detained patients relate of course to treatment for the mental disorder necessitating the patient's detention. They do not apply to treatment for other conditions. So far as these conditions are concerned a detained patient is in the same position as a non-psychiatric patient and the doctor should be able to impose only such treatment without the patient's consent as is immediately necessary to preserve the patient's life or health. This is the advice currently given by the Medical Defence Societies. There will be some patients, particularly the severely mentally handicapped, who will be incapable of giving valid consent even to routine medical treatment. In these cases it would clearly not be right for the hospital to withhold such treatment until an emergency arises, nor would it always be appropriate for a guardian to be appointed to give or withhold consent on the patient's behalf. Clearly, in these circumstances some reliance must be placed on professional judgment in providing routine medication for minor illnesses. Where more serious medical intervention is required and need is not in doubt, the best course would seem

74

to be for the nearest relative to be consulted, but if there is no relative, or there is doubt about the treatment, the views of the proposed multi-disciplinary panel (see paragraphs 6.28 and 6.29 below) should be obtained.

*Different forms of treatment*

6.25   The different forms of psychiatric treatment which are considered to warrant special arrangements fall in principle into three groups—

    i. treatments which necessitate the removal or destruction of brain tissue or are designed to effect irreversible change in cerebral or bodily functions—subsequently referred to in this Paper as 'irreversible' treatments;

    ii. treatments where the risk of adverse reaction or the severity of such reaction would be disproportionate to the degree of benefit the treatment is likely to confer or the prospect of success—subsequently referred to as 'hazardous'; and

    iii. treatments not in general use or whose safety and efficacy have not yet been confirmed by clinical research (subsequently referred to as 'treatments not fully established').

The concern which is felt about these sorts of treatment suggests that before they are given or imposed a second opinion—the nature of which is discussed in paragraphs 6.28 and 6.29 below—should always be sought except where the treatment is urgently needed to save life. There may be doubt about whether a particular treatment is irreversible, hazardous or not fully established, and in this case also a second opinion should be sought. Moreover, where a detained patient is capable of giving a valid consent, such treatment should not, in any circumstances other than to save life, be administered without both his express consent and a concurring second opinion. Paragraph 1.14, above, proposed that such treatments should not be given to informal patients who have consented without a second opinion being obtained.

6.26   Whether a particular treatment is considered to be 'hazardous' and so to require a second opinion would depend upon the circumstances of the individual case. The doctor responsible would have to consider the potential risks of the procedure and balance these against the severity of the patient's disorder and the prospect of benefit from the treatment. The Government is conscious that there is public anxiety about the use, and alleged abuse in some cases, of electro-convulsive therapy (ECT) and that many will want to know how its use in the treatment of detained patients would be affected by an arrangement such as that being suggested. The Royal College of Psychiatrists* published a report on ECT last year which contained a review of the scientific evidence of its effectiveness and of any adverse effects. This indicated that, whilst there is substantial evidence of its effectiveness in the treatment of severe endogenous depressive illness, it may be less effective as a treatment for other conditions; and that its use may involve some risk to the patient (mainly from the muscle relaxant and the anaesthetic). If, therefore, proposals on the lines of those above were adopted, the question whether ECT was 'hazardous' would depend

---

* The Royal College of Psychiatrists' 'Memorandum on the Use of Electroconvulsive Therapy'. *Brit. J. Psychiat. (1977). 131*, 261–272.

on the individual case including the type and severity of the mental illness. In most cases of severe endogenous depression its use would not be regarded as 'hazardous' unless there were contra-indications from a physical condition. In other cases, however, the balance of benefit against risk might be different. Alternative treatments (eg those involving drugs) may of course present equal or even greater risks and promise less by way of benefit; all such factors will need to be taken into account by the consultant in charge of the patient's treatment and those called in to give a second opinion.

## Patients detained for short periods

6.27   It was suggested in the Consultative Document* that the treatment which it should be permissible to impose on patients detained under section 25 of the Act should be more limited than for patients detained under section 26, since the latter has at present more safeguards than section 25. The Government now proposes however (paragraph 2.12, above) that section 25 should be recognised as an assessment and treatment order and that new safeguards should be introduced. In consequence, no separate arrangements would be necessary for patients detained under section 25. It is not considered appropriate to authorise the compulsory treatment of patients detained under section 29, though such treatment as is required in emergency to restrain violence or to save life is of course covered by common law. Patients subject to the other emergency powers (sections 30, 135 and 136) are detained in hospital or removed to a place of safety to enable examination and provide time pending authorisation of longer term powers, and there should be no question of imposing treatment, other than treatment needed immediately to save life or to control a violent episode.

## The form of the second opinion

6.28   The need for a second opinion to be sought when certain categories of treatment are being proposed was supported by the general consensus of opinion following the discussion of this in the Consultative Document, but while there was general recognition of the need to seek a second opinion in certain circumstances, there was less agreement on the form it should take. The Consultative Document** suggested that a second opinion might be obtained in one of three ways: (i) an independent psychiatrist's opinion; (ii) from a Committee in each hospital charged with oversight of the Rights and Responsibilities of Staff and Patients; (iii) from a multi-disciplinary panel especially established for the purpose. There was a good deal of support for the multi-disciplinary panel on the ground that this would add a new and important safeguard in relation to contentious treatments. Much, but not all, medical opinion was against the introduction of multi-disciplinary panels, but it is hoped that, in the light of the widespread support for them, the medical profession will feel able to go along with this proposal. The Government believes that the establishment of such panels with a substantial medical involvement would bring positive advantages and it is proposed that arrangements should be made for them to be set up. It is proposed that having sought the opinion of the panel it should not be permissible to impose treatment except with the panel's endorsement.

* Para 8.29.
** Paras 8.25 to 8.27.

6.29 The Consultative Document left open the questions whether the panel should be a hospital , area or regional panel and who the members should be. There was very little comment on either point. Although the volume of work likely to fall to such panels cannot be estimated precisely, it seems unlikely to be enough to justify a panel in each hospital. In any case, it might not then be thought sufficiently independent of the psychiatric team involved with the patient's treatment in the same hospital. On the other hand, a regional panel would probably be too distant; and an area panel would seem the most appropriate. It is proposed that, in addition to medical and other professional members, the panel should include a lay member.

## Rights of patients

6.30 Patients should be given information about their rights, and the limitations of those rights, at the time they enter hospital, and about any change in legal status. They should also be given information about their rights to refuse treatment, the limitations on those rights in respect of detained patients and their rights to ask for a second opinion. They should be aware, as indeed should staff, of the general principles outlined in paragraph 6.18, above. It is proposed to issue guidance recommending hospital managers to provide patients and staff with information about patients' rights in these respects and advising any member of staff who proposes to impose treatment on a detained patient without his consent to make sure first, unless it is an emergency, that the patient is aware of his rights in relation to a second opinion.

## OTHER SAFEGUARDS

6.31 The Consultative Document* discussed a number of other suggestions for further safeguards for patients—the Butler Committee's suggestion of a scheme of 'patients' friends'; the Royal College of Psychiatrists' suggestion of a Mental Welfare Commission on the lines of the Scottish one; and MIND's suggestion of an advocacy scheme. Since the 1959 Mental Health Act there have been a number of developments aimed at improving the position of patients, many of them for patients in general but including those suffering from mental disorder. Notable among these are the introduction of Community Health Councils and of the Commissioners for Local Government and the NHS (the Ombudsmen). Another is the Health Advisory Service (formerly called the Hospital Advisory Service) with its special remit in relation to psychiatric services. In addition, there are the Davies Committee's recommendations for improving complaints procedures. A Development Team for the Mentally Handicapped has also been set up, though this is concerned with advice on services rather than patients' individual rights. The Consultative Document suggested a further safeguard by means of a scheme of 'patients' advisers' whose function it would be to advise patients of their rights generally and about procedural matters, for example the proper way to make any complaint that they have and how to apply to a Mental Health Review Tribunal. The Document suggested that a limited number of trial schemes might be set up and their usefulness evaluated.

---

* Para 8.38 to 8.48.

6.32 There was much support for this suggestion, but not for a formal advocacy system which was generally regarded as unwarranted. The appointment of patients' friends for all detained patients also lacked support—for the reason which the Butler Committee itself acknowledged, that it would be extremely difficult to find enough interested people of the right calibre.

6.33 There was also only limited support for the establishment of mental welfare commissions on the lines of the Scottish Mental Welfare Commission but since this is an arrangement which seems to be functioning well in Scotland it is perhaps necessary to explain in more detail why the Government does not propose to introduce such a scheme in England and Wales. Those who favour the introduction of mental welfare commissions argue that it is not realistic to have common arrangements for safeguarding the position of psychiatric patients and other NHS patients since much of the psychiatric service is, and will continue for some time to be, separate from general NHS services and since the compulsory powers which are available in relation to psychiatric patients make them different from the vast majority of other NHS patients. They therefore see attractions in bringing together the various protective functions under a single body, thus making it simpler for patients and for staff to know to whom to turn if a problem arises. The Royal College of Psychiatrists argue that the role of Mental Health Review Tribunals should be expanded and merged into that of new bodies which would also undertake functions analogous to those of the Scottish Mental Welfare Commission.

6.34 The Government considers that the Royal Commission's aim that psychiatric patients should, to the fullest extent practicable, be treated in the same way as non-psychiatric patients should remain a guiding principle in legislation and in the provision of services. As paragraph 6.31 above, points out, a number of developments in the past decade have given patients in general opportunities to make known their views on services and to have any complaints adequately considered. If mental welfare commissions were to be introduced for psychiatric patients, there would seem little point in continuing to apply to them the various arrangements now available to all patients. Mental welfare commissions in England and Wales would have to draw on scarce manpower resources—medical manpower in particular— and would have considerable financial implications—these have been estimated at £2 million per year at current prices. More importantly, it is thought wrong in principle to reintroduce a system for psychiatric patients which is fundamentally different from that for other patients.

6.35 The Government's view is that the most important factor in safeguarding the position of vulnerable patients and ensuring that their rights are upheld is personal contact between the patient and someone whose job it is to explain the position from the patient's own point of view and that the introduction of another system of complaints procedure or of another 'watchdog' organisation is not the answer. The Government therefore proposes to try out a limited number of experimental schemes of patients' advisers. It wishes to emphasise that these should in no way be taken as a criticism of the staff who look after patients but as a recognition that some patients may have lost their initiative to act in their own best interest or to seek discharge from hospital or hostel, and may need encouragement and support which hard-pressed staff are unable to provide on an individual basis. It is hoped that the trial schemes will have the full co-operation of all concerned. The schemes will of course need to be evaluated to see how useful they prove to be.

## SUMMARY OF PROPOSALS: CHAPTER 6

### Mental Health Review Tribunals

i.   Opportunities for detained patients to refer their cases to a Tribunal and for detained patients under a restriction order to ask for their cases to be referred to a Tribunal should be increased in line with the proposed reductions in the periods of detention (except that patients under a restriction order should not have a right to request reference to a Tribunal within the first 12 months) (para 6.2).

ii.   Automatic reviews by Mental Health Review Tribunals should be introduced for unrestricted patients. These should take place after 6 months, then within three years of admission and at three-yearly intervals thereafter (para 6.3).

iii.   The Home Secretary should be required to refer the case of a restricted patient automatically to a Tribunal at the end of any 3 year period in which the case has not been otherwise referred (para 6.3).

iv.   Powers should be taken in the Act further to reduce these periods by regulation if this proves practicable and desirable in the light of experience (para 6.3).

v.   Tribunals should be able to order delayed discharge (for up to three months) (para 6.5).

vi.   Tribunals should be able to recommend trial leave, transfer to another hospital or to guardianship and should receive reports on these; and be able to make an alternative finding if their recommendations cannot be implemented (para 6.5).

vii.   An application should not be withdrawn without the permission of the Tribunal and withdrawal should not prevent a further application being made in the specified period (para 6.6).

viii.   Greater use should be made of members with social services experience and a fourth member of the Tribunal should be appointed where appropriate. Forensic psychiatrists should be included on the medical panel where possible (paras 6.7 and 6.8).

ix.   Tribunals should continue to be involved in reviewing the detention of restricted patients (para 6.11).

x.   Automatic reference to a Tribunal should be made when a restricted patient is recalled to hospital and should be done within a month of recall (para 6.12).

xi.   The current review of Tribunal procedures may lead to further changes of detail in the Act (para 6.13).

*Consent to treatment*

xii.   There is no provision in the 1959 act either authorising or implying that treatment can be imposed on an *informal* patient without his consent. No change in this position is contemplated (para 6.15).

xiii.   The Act should be amended to make it clear that staff may in certain circumstances (as well as in an emergency) treat a *detained* patient for his mental disorder without his consent. But this should apply only to patients *detained* under sections 25, 26 or 60* and not to those detained under sections 29, 30, 135 or 136 (paras 6.16–6.21 and 6.27).

xiv.   Treatment not relating to the mental disorder should not be imposed on a detained patient without his consent, other than such treatment as is immediately necessary to preserve his life or health (para 6.24).

xv.   Treatment which is irreversible, hazardous or not fully established should not be imposed without the patient's consent (except to save life), and, even if the patient (whether informal or detained) does give consent, treatment should not be administered without a concurring second opinion (paras 6.23 and 6.25).

xvi.   A second opinion should be sought where there is doubt as to whether a particular form of treatment is irreversible, hazardous or not fully established (para 6.25).

xvii.   Where a detained patient is capable of giving a valid consent (ie of understanding the nature, purpose and likely effects of the treatment proposed) his consent to treatment should always be sought (other than in an emergency). If he refuses, the consultant should seek an alternative form of treatment to which the patient will agree. But if the patient still refuses and the treatment is considered by the consultant to be necessary to save the patient's life, prevent violence or prevent deterioration of the patient's mental condition, a concurring second opinion should be obtained before carrying out the treatment. The treatment selected should be that which is least objectionable to the patient or which represents the minimum interference with him (paras 6.18 to 6.21 and 6.23).

xviii.   If a detained patient is not capable of giving a valid consent, the consultant should be able to carry out such treatment as he considers necessary to alleviate or cure the mental disorder (other than irreversible, hazardous or not fully established treatments) (para 6.23).

xix.   Where, except in an emergency, there is uncertainty about whether a patient's refusal is based on an adequate understanding of the nature, purpose and likely effects of the treatment proposed, a second opinion should be sought, and if he is considered capable of this understanding, whether his refusal should be overridden (para 6.23).

xx.   The second opinion referred to in xv, xvi, xvii and xix above should be obtained from a multidisciplinary panel especially established for the purpose by each Area Health Authority (para 6.28 and 6.29).

xxi.   It should be the duty of hospital managers to inform patients of their rights in respect of consent to treatment including their right to refuse consent or to ask for a second opinion (para 6.30).

---

* This would include people detained as if under section 60, eg section 72 patients.

*Further protection of patients' rights*

xxii.   Rather than a system of advocates or of " 'patients' friends' ", as suggested by the Butler Committee, a limited number of experimental schemes of patients' advisers should be set up. A Mental Welfare Commission on Scottish lines should not be introduced (para 6.35).

## CHAPTER 7

# SAFEGUARDS FOR STAFF

SECTION 141

7.1   Section 141 provides that civil or criminal proceedings against a person acting or purporting to act in pursuance of the Mental Health Act can be brought only with the leave of the High Court. In granting leave the High Court must be satisfied that there is substantial ground for the contention that the person concerned acted in bad faith or without reasonable care, This applies not only to hospital staff but to any other person involved in admission or discharge procedures, including doctors, social workers, relatives—and also police officers acting in pursuance of sections 135 or 136.

7.2   The Consultative Document* discussed various criticisms of the section, notably that it is an unwarranted restriction on access to the courts in that it is not founded on any evidence that psychiatric patients are likely to be vexatious litigants. Indeed, MIND** argue that experience over the years shows that psychiatric patients seldom resort to legal action. On the other hand, the Government is aware of staff anxiety about their legal position.

7.3   Staff anxiety seems to have increased in recent years and is highlighted in the Document published in September 1977 by the Confederation of Health Service Employees (COHSE), *'The Management of Violent or Potentially Violent Patients'*. There are a number of respects in which staff are unsure of their legal position and anxious in case a slight mistake may lay them open to the possibility of prosecution. Such difficulties are particularly likely to arise in administering treatment to patients who become disturbed and potentially violent and who may require restraint, detention or seclusion; and in searching patients for potentially dangerous items, alcohol and untaken drugs. The Government accepts that there is a need for the law to be more specific in these areas. It is suggested in paragraphs 2.29 to 2.32, above, that section 30 of the Act should be amended to enable a suitably qualified nurse to have a holding power for up to six hours to give time to enable a formal application for detention to be made. This should reduce uncertainty nursing staff may have over their legal position in managing a patient who suddenly becomes very difficult or violent or who wishes to leave hospital but would be likely if he did so to be a danger to himself or others. Paragraphs 6.14 to 6.30, above, set out the Government's proposals in relation to consent to treatment. These would give staff specific powers to impose treatment on patients but in specified circumstances and subject to clear limitations; and it is hoped that these proposals will remove the present uncertainty about arrangements for consent to treatment. Paragraphs 7.12 to 7.16, below, discuss the position on right to search

*   Paras 9.1 to 9.8.
**  'A Human Condition'. Vol I, pp. 104–110.

and make it clear that staff would have a defence under common law in searching both patients and their property where there is cause to believe that an emergency might arise. These paragraphs suggest, however, that the common law position is less clear in relation to situations which cannot be identified as emergencies but where there is cause to believe that an emergency might arise; guidance clarifying the position is proposed.

7.4 The Goverment recognises the need to retain some 'long stop' provision of this sort to reassure staff that they will not be involved unnecessarily in ill-founded court cases—to have to appear in court can be a difficult and stressful experience—but absolute protection against the very few litigious patients cannot be achieved without an unacceptable loss of rights for all patients. The Government therefore proposes some changes to simplify and clarify the present position. It hopes that if such changes are made staff will feel on surer ground and that improvements from the point of view of the patients will be acceptable. The comments received on the Consultative Document encourage this hope.

*Removal of criminal action from section 141*

7.5 The Consultative Document* suggested that criminal actions should be removed from the scope of section 141 and made subject to provisions similar to those in section 126 concerning ill-treatment of patients. This would mean that the Director of Public Prosecutions, rather than the High Court, would have to give leave before criminal proceedings could be taken against a member of staff in relation to actions taken in the course of his duties. This suggestion was widely endorsed by a number of staff and professional bodies, and the Government proposes to adopt it in amending legislation. Section 141 would then only apply to civil actions. It is worth noting that, since employing authorities are usually liable for the acts of employees, civil actions for damages are usually directed against the employer rather than against individual members of staff.

*Civil actions: substitution of 'reasonable' for 'substantial'*

7.6 The Consultative Document also suggested that section 141 should be amended so as to require 'reasonable' rather than 'substantial' grounds for the contention that the defendant acted in bad faith or without reasonable care. It pointed out that this was similar to the provision in the Northern Ireland Mental Health Act, which requires only that a 'prima facie' case should be established and whose operation seems to have resulted in no difficulty.

7.7 Only a very small number of applications (four or five a year) are made for leave to proceed under section 141 though the difficulty of making an application may be a contributory factor. However, even if the restrictions were to be eased, there is no reason to suppose that this would result in a large increase in the number of actions against staff. The proposal to amend 'substantial' to 'reasonable' received a good deal of support, largely on the ground that the requirement to establish 'substantial ground' before the High Court means in practice that the patient has virtually to

* Para 9.13.

prove his case in advance. On the other hand, some staff organisations believe that a change of this sort would lessen a safeguard against unfounded accusations against staff and would seriously undermine morale, particularly where staff deal with disturbed or aggressive patients.

*The scope of section 141*

7.8    The Consultative Document* pointed out that, although it is clear that section 141 applies to actions arising out of the control of a detained patient, for example the use of physical restraint or seclusion, it is less clear whether it also applies to the treatment of a detained patient or to the treatment or control of an informal patient. The Government has now received legal advice on these matters, which is that section 141 does apply to both the treatment and the control of detained patients but that it is not clear whether it extends to the treatment or control of informal patients. Such uncertainty is obviously unsatisfactory and it is proposed to clarify the position in amending legislation.

7.9    If, as is proposed in paragraphs 6.14 to 6.30, above, the Act is amended to give power to impose treatment on detained patients in certain circumstances, section 141 should clearly apply to staff who give treatment to those patients within those circumstances; and it is proposed that this should be made explicit in legislation.

7.10    There is nowadays general agreement that the position of informal psychiatric patients should be as close as possible to that of non-psychiatric hospital patients. It follows that section 141 should not apply to informal patients. Paragraph 6.15, above, makes it clear that there is no power to treat informal patients against their will except in emergencies, nor is it proposed to take such a power. So far as control is concerned, as distinct from treatment, it seems better to rely on the defence afforded by the common law for emergencies and on the proposed extension of section 30 than to extend the scope of section 141. The Government therefore proposes to make it clear in amending legislation that the scope of section 141 does not apply to the control or treatment of informal patients.

*Administrative guidance*

7.11    There was considerable support for the suggestion in the Consultative Document** that adminstrative action should be taken to ensure that staff have as much detailed information as possible as to their legal position and on how they can ensure that they do not unwittingly contravene the law. The Government hopes that more detailed guidance to staff on difficult areas where there is doubt—such as consent to treatment, the right of search, etc.—will contribute to this and it is intended that guidance will be issued following amending legislation.

THE RIGHT TO SEARCH PATIENTS AND THEIR BELONGINGS AND TO WITHHOLD ITEMS IN THE INTERESTS OF SECURITY

7.12    The Consultative Document*** suggested that new powers to withhold items in the interest of security were not required, since legal advice

---

*    Paras 9.4 and 9.5.
**   Para 9.12.
*** Para 10.28.

84

to the Department of Health and Social Security was that staff already have authority at common law and by virtue of section 3(1) of the Criminal Law Act 1967 to take reasonable measures to prevent a patient from keeping in his possession articles of potential danger (eg matches, weapons, alcohol, tools, explosives, etc.). This opinion had been set out in official guidance (HC(76)11) and it was hoped that this would reassure staff about their right to take such measures. Most comments on the Document agreed that no new powers were necessary. However, the COHSE document—*'The Management of Violent or Potentially Violent Patients'*—makes it clear that COHSE members did not find the official guidance in circular HC(76)11 sufficiently reassuring. The following is an extract from the COHSE document:

'83.1  The position in law of the right of staff is less than clear and we believe that the 1959 Act should be amended to include certain powers. Legal advice suggests that searches for dangerous weapons may only be carried out by a police officer and a search for drugs may only be carried out under the provisions of the Misuse of Drugs Act, 1971. It has been suggested, however, that staff *do* have the legal right to search a *detained* patient although nowhere does such an express provision appear in the 1959 Act.

83.2  Informal patients may be discharged if they refuse to consent to be searched; while a hospital rule making search compulsory if requested would have no standing in law, the sanction of discharge for refusal to consent may always be used and in the case of many patients would be likely to be effective.

83.3  Searches of clothing in order to find out whether a patient has been taking a prescribed course of drugs, however, while quite common in a psychiatric hospital today, is probably not lawful.

83.4  Search of a section patient or his property would probably be justified if reasonable cause existed to believe that he was armed and therefore a danger to others or likely to use the weapon to assist in absconding. Informal patients may be made subject to a Section 30(2) order if necessary and justifiable . . .

83.5  The Confederation will seek an amendment to the 1959 Act allowing specifificially authorised persons to search the person and property of patients in their charge where reasonable cause exists.'

7.13  In the light of the uncertainty expressed, the Government has looked again at the official guidance already given. It seems generally accepted that staff acting reasonably in cases of emergency are likely to have a good defence if a case is brought against them, and will have the support both of their employing authority and of their union or staff association. On the other hand, it also seems clear that there is no legal justification for a routine search of a patient's belongings where there is no particular indication of potential violence or danger from the patient concerned. However, although violence or danger may not be immediately present, staff may have good grounds for believing that there is a real risk that this may arise. They may have good reason to suspect for example that a patient has concealed a dangerous weapon or drugs or alcohol. At present there appears to be little legal authority for a member of staff to search a patient's property and/or person simply to establish whether there is a risk of violence or danger, and it is understandable in these circumstances that staff are anxious about taking such action, however necessary they might feel it to be.

7.14   The Government has therefore reconsidered whether new, specific powers of search should be introduced in order to remove this uncertainty. There are certainly attractions in having, as COHSE has suggested, a power for a nominated member of staff to undertake searches. There would however be difficulties, both practical and philosophical, in so doing. To be of real use to staff the power would need to relate to informal as well as to detained patients for it is here that the uncertainties are greatest. But it is doubtful whether such a statutory provision could be drafted satisfactorily. COHSE's suggestion, for example, is for a power to search in cases 'where reasonable cause exists' and some such qualifying phrase would seem essential. Yet such a qualification could be open to as much dispute and give rise to as much uncertainty as does the present situation. Conversely, to attempt to draft the provision to define the specific situations in which searches would be permissible would also be likely to prove unsatisfactory and indeed, if circumstances arose which required a search but which had not been foreseen by the legislators, might make the position of staff even more difficult. The Government's view therefore is that it would be better not to attempt to introduce new statutory powers of search.

7.15   The difficulties of staff are, however, fully recognized as is the need to give clear guidance on the scope and limitations of existing powers. It can of course be explained to patients why there is a need to make occasional searches and to seek their co-operation in the interests of safety. Recent years have given ample evidence that, in general, members of the public are prepared to comply with such procedures—at airports, theatres, museums etc.

7.16   It is proposed that guidance should be issued to authorities on how searches might be mounted. Such guidance would set out as clearly as possible the scope and limitations of legal protection for staff and would suggest procedural safeguards to help staff in the event of complaints. These safeguards will need to be discussed with the professional and staff associations concerned but would be likely to consist of arrangements for the approval of searches by at least one senior officer; for the recording of searches in a report book and for informing patients that their belongings are to be, or have been, searched. It would seem advisable for patients to be present whilst their belongings are searched.

OTHER FACTORS WHICH AFFECT STAFF

7.17   Changes in the law relating to the giving of treatment and the detention of disturbed patients, together with the protection of the kind afforded by section 141 and a clearer understanding of the right to search, should go a long way towards reassuring staff. But this is no substitute for adequate staffing levels and facilities. It is recognised that insufficient nursing cover on the ward, for example, can make it difficult and even hazardous for staff to cope with violent incidents. It can also make it more likely that such incidents will occur since potential problems will not be identified and tackled at an early stage. When staff are called upon to deal with the small minority of patients who need to be treated under close supervision or some degree of security they are naturally anxious that there should be appropriate facilities and enough staff to adequately manage the patients. How these problems are dealt with is a matter for local management to decide in consultation with staff interests. There may be a need to deploy extra staffing as and when required on particular wards or to set aside permanently some ward—or beds—with above-average staff to deal with crises as they arise.

7.18   It is hoped that the establishment of regional secure psychiatric units will help in dealing with this problem both by providing a specialist service and by developing centres of expertise in dealing with difficult or violent patients, so playing an active part as a source of advice and training for staff in other psychiatric services in the region.

7.19   Employing authorities have, of course, a general responsibility under the Health and Safety at Work Act 1974 to ensure, so far as is reasonably practicable, the safety of the working environment of their employees and need to ensure that staff have such information, training and supervision as is needed to achieve this objective.

### SUMMARY OF PROPOSALS: CHAPTER 7

*Section 141*

i.   Section 141 should be retained but criminal actions should be removed from its scope and made subject to leave to proceed from the Director of Public Prosecutions instead of the High Court (para 7.5).

ii.   in section 141(2) the word 'substantial' should be replaced by 'reasonable' (paras 7.6 and 7.7).

iii.   the section should be clarified to ensure that it covers treatment imposed on detained patients provided such treatment is in accordance with the treatment arrangements set out in Chapter 6 (para 7.9).

iv.   it should be made clear that section 141 does not apply to informal psychiatric patients (para 7.10).

v.   further guidance should be issued to clarify the legal position of staff in difficult areas such as treatment of patients (para 7.11).

*Right to search*

vi.   statutory powers to search informal patients should not be introduced; instead guidance should be issued setting out the scope and limitations of legal protection for staff and suggesting procedural safeguards (para 7.16).

# CHAPTER 8

# OTHER MATTERS

## PATIENTS' MAIL

8.1   At present under section 36 of the Act, in-coming mail may be withheld from a detained patient on the authority of the Responsible Medical Officer where its receipt would be calculated, in the opinion of the Responsible Medical Officer, to interfere with the patient's treatment or to cause him unnecessary distress. The section also allows a patient's out-going mail to be intercepted if it appears to the Responsible Medical Officer that it would be unreasonably offensive to the addressee or is defamatory of other persons (other than the staff of the hospital). Out-going mail to certain people or groups of people specified in the section (eg MPs) is exempt from these powers of interception. Where an individual has given notice in writing to the managers of the hospital or to the Responsible Medical Officer asking that communications addressed to him by the patient should be withheld then they may be so withheld. Section 134 of the Act applies the provisions of section 36 to informal patients. The provisions also apply to persons who are under guardianship, the place of the Responsible Medical Officer being taken by the guardian.

8.2   These powers are wider than those recommended by the Royal Commission which said that 'there should be no censorship of out-going letters from patients (whether subject to detention or not) except at the request of individual addressees'*; also, the Commission expected that the power to withhold in-coming mail would be used sparingly. The Consultative Document** drew attention to this and noted a number of criticisms of existing provisions.*** Essentially, these criticisms were that the exercise of these powers was at the sole discretion of the Responsible Medical Officer who was thus called upon to make judgements on non-medical matters, that the rights of all patients could be infringed because of the needs of a few and that communication which could be of therapeutic value might be discouraged. The Consultative Document argued, however, that as no serious problems seemed to have arisen in practice the powers should be retained, subject to the introduction of a requirement that patients be informed if their mail was examined or withheld and to the addition of the European Commission of Human Rights and CHCs to the list of bodies in section 36(2) with whom patients' correspondence must be unhindered.

8.3   The Government notes that the Northern Ireland Mental Health Act contains no provision for withholding correspondence and that this has not given rise to problems.

---

\*    Cmnd 169. Para 299.
\*\*   Paras 10.29 to 10.31.
\*\*\* '*A Human Condition*'. Vol I, pp. 111–114.

8.4 Arguments in favour of retaining powers to withhold correspondence seem to rest essentially on grounds either of security or of potential distress to the patient or addressee. These considerations need perhaps to be examined separately in relation to informal and detained patients and also in relation to the particular circumstances of Special Hospital patients.

*Informal patients*

8.5 The question of security does not arise in relation to informal patients; and any justification for distinguishing between such patients and non-psychiatric patients (whose mail, of course, is not subject to any restrictions), as regards withholding incoming correspondence, the possibility that they might receive letters which distress them or have a disruptive effect on their treatment. In practice, however, the pattern of modern communications—in, for instance, use of the telephone—is now such that withholding correspondence would be sealing off only one form of communication and is unlikely to be effective in isolating informal patients from distressing or disruptive information. It is questionable, also, whether it is helpful to protect such patients, most of whom nowadays only stay in hospital for a few weeks or even days, from distressing news or conflicting viewpoints which they are in any event likely to encounter on discharge.

8.6 Hospital practice, also, has changed significantly. Shorter and repeated admissions, the marked increase in out-patient and day-patient treatment and the sharing of day hospital services by in-patients and day-patients have blurred the distinction between in-patients and other patients. Increasingly, patients are being treated in psychiatric units in general hospitals, and freedom of movement of patients in these units, and in traditional psychiatric hospitals, is now widespread. These factors make it difficult to exercise effective control over patients' correspondence.

8.7 Out-going letters from patients which might cause distress to recipients would seem to provide the main argument for considering a form of control. Psychiatric patients are of course not the only people who might send such letters, and there is no sound evidence that they display a propensity towards this. Indeed some patients, for example the mentally handicapped, may be considerably less capable of composing distressing or abusive correspondence than others. Concern on these grounds in relation to a small minority of patients does not seem sufficient to counter the arguments against depriving the vast majority of patients of a right to unhindered correspondence, nor to justify setting up elaborate machinery to overcome the practical difficulties of exercising effective control over the correspondence of informal patients.

8.8 In the light of the above, the Government considers that there are insufficient arguments for retaining powers to withhold the mail of informal psychiatric patients, and proposes that section 134 should be repealed.

*Detained patients*

8.9 Most of the above arguments apply also to detained patients and persons under guardianship. Most detained patients in local psychiatric hospitals do not need to be treated under conditions of strict security, and there is ordinarily no justification for inspecting their mail on grounds of security. (The position of patients in Special Hospitals and secure units is discussed below in paragraphs 8.12 to 8.17.) Moreover, patients subject to compulsory detention are in practice detained for only a short period, and many have considerable freedom to come and go and to receive visitors. Nor does there seem to be any basis for assuming that detained patients are more likely to be upset by incoming correspondence than other patients. Indeed, it has been argued that the fact that mail may be withheld, and that the patient is not required to be informed if it has, can itself be upsetting to patients (and their correspondents). It is proposed therefore to remove the present power to withhold the in-coming mail of detained patients and of persons under guardianship.

8.10   There are similar difficulties over out-going mail. It is not possible to intercept all correspondence which might be offensive since there are alternative methods of sending letters, such as persuading informal patients to post them. Nor is there evidence that detained patients are more likely to write abusive or distressing letters than other patients. There may however be a small number of cases where a patient's letter would be particularly distressing to its intended recipient, for example where a patient who has committed a serious crime writes to his victim or to the victim's relatives; and it seems right to attempt to exercise such control as is practicable in such cases. It is therefore proposed that it should remain possible for the hospital authorities to withhold out-going mail addressed to somebody who has specifically requested that mail addressed to him by a detained patient or a person under guardianship should not be sent to him. Such mail would be returned to the patient who would be entitled to assume that, otherwise, his mail was not being intercepted or interfered with in any way.

8.11   If detained patients are to have an unhindered right to send letters, with the exception noted in the preceding paragraph, there would no longer seem to be a need for the list in section 36(2)(b) of persons and organisations to whom patients may write without fear of interception. The Government proposes, therefore, to retain only section 36(2)(a), which provides for the withholding of correspondence from a detained patient or a person under guardianship at the request of the addressee, and to repeal the rest of section 36.

### Special Hospitals and secure units

8.12   As it stands, section 36 does not provide for withholding mail on grounds of security: the Consultative Document* noted the view of DHSS legal advisers that staff have authority at common law and by virtue of section 3(1) of the Criminal Law Act 1967 to take reasonable measures to prevent a patient from receiving or keeping in his possession articles of potential danger. Nevertheless, a main concern of Special Hospitals is security and it is felt by staff at those hospitals that there is a need for a power to intercept correspondence, especially since the very existence of such a power might constitute a considerable deterrent to those seeking to plan escapes or obtain money or articles useful in an escape or dangerous in themselves. Similar considerations will be important in the regional secure psychiatric units as these become established.

---

* Para 10.28.

8.13  It has been argued that, in some cases, the opening, inspection and possible confiscation of letters, articles or money in front of a patient might be very disturbing for him, and it might be preferable if the inspection of mail took place elsewhere. It may also be administratively convenient if all inspection is carried out at a central point. At the same time, it would be unlikely to be necessary from a security point of view to make the opening of all mail a matter of routine and the Government feels that this would unnecessarily restrict the rights of patients. Inspection of mail and the retention of items on grounds of security should be the responsibility of the hospital managers with power to designate officers to undertake this function on their behalf. The criterion to be applied when considering withholding items on grounds of security should be the interests of the patient's safety or the protection of other persons.

8.14  Patients should be told when their mail is being inspected and informed within 24 hours of any item withheld and a record should be kept of any delay in delivery and of any items withheld. Where an item is withheld the patient should have a right to appeal to the hospital managers—such an appeal should be heard within 14 days.

8.15  It is also considered that such patients should be free to write without hindrance to responsible individuals or organisations who are acting on their behalf in various capacities. It is proposed that powers to inspect or withhold postal packets should not apply to letters from patients to any of the individuals or organisations specified below—

i. the Secretaries of State for Social Services and for Wales and the Home Secretary;
ii. Members of Parliament;
iii. the Master and Deputy Master of the Court of Protection;
iv. the Parliamentary Commissioner for Administration, the Health Service Commissioner and the Commissioners for Local Administration;
v. the hospital managers;
vi. any Mental Health Review Tribunal to which the patient is entitled to make application;
vii. any authority or person who has the power to discharge the patient;
viii. Community Health Councils;
ix. the European Commission of Human Rights;
x. the patient's nearest relative;
xi. the patient's solicitor.

8.16  In the case of in-coming mail from the individuals or organisations listed the hospital managers will want to be satisfied, for security purposes, that mail does come from its purported source. The Government proposes, therefore, that the hospital managers should have power to inspect in-coming mail, when this is essential to confirm that it is from one of the individuals and organisations listed.

8.17  It is considered advisable also to apply the arrangements outlined above to regional secure psychiatric units.

8.18   Under section 40(3) the period in which a detained patient who absconds from hospital can be compulsorily returned is limited. If he is not subject to a restriction order under section 65 it is limited to 28 days from the date of absconding (six months in the case of a patient over 21 suffering from psychopathic disorder or subnormality). This period applies irrespective of the date of expiry of the original period of detention. Detained patients subject to a restriction order can be compulsorily returned to hospital at any time. The Butler Committee thought that the reasons for allowing only 28 days for the return of a patient were no longer valid.* They noted that in practice relatively little attempt is made to trace absconding patients and that sometimes, when the whereabouts of a missing patient remain unknown, it is because of the kindness of friends rather than because the patient is capable of living independently. They recommended a more flexible system under which compulsory return could be enforced at any time before the end of the current period of detention. They thought however that it should be for the Responsible Medical Officer to decide whether or not to require the return of an absconding patient since they could see little medical or social purpose in enforcing the return to hospital of a patient who would not co-operate with treatment, and who presented no danger to the public. MIND have suggested** that section 40(3) should not apply to section 60 patients (offender patients) and that they should be subject to compulsory return indefinitely. Behind this suggestion is the fear that a court might impose a restriction order in addition to a hospital order if it thought there was a risk that the offender would abscond from hospital and could then not be compulsorily returned after he had been absent for only 28 days.

8.19   The Consultive Document*** suggested that, if the Butler recommendations were to be accepted, some arrangement should be retained to cover the case of a patient who absconds shortly before his detention is due to end. It proposed a maximum period—say six months from the date of absconding— during which the patient could be compulsorily returned. The Document went on to suggest that, within those limits, the question of return should be left to the discretion of the Responsible Medical Officer as the Butler Committee suggested. However, in cases where he did not consider it necessary to seek the patient's return he should be required formally to discharge him as soon as possible, perhaps within a week of his absconding. Very few comments were received on this question.

8.20   On further consideration however it is felt that the proposal in the Document may result in complications for the staff and for the police who would have to operate the system and also that a period of 6 months may be too long. The Government has therefore reconsidered the matter and sets out fresh proposals below.

8.21   Section 40(3) at present applies, in addition to the longer term powers which were the concern of the Butler Committee, to patients who

---

\*      Cmnd 6244. Paras 14.13, 14.14 and 14.16.
\*\*    'A Human Condition'. Vol 2, pp. 41–42.
\*\*\*  Paras 10.4 to 10.6.

are subject to short term powers of detention (sections 29, 25 and 30(2)). Since those powers are intentionally of short duration and the need for longer term detention has not been established there seems little justification for providing for compulsory return to hospital beyond the life of those powers; if the patient needs to be compulsorily returned to hospital this would be best achieved by making a fresh order. It is therefore proposed that the Act should be amended so that section 40(3) would no longer apply to short term power.

8.22 As far as the longer term powers (sections 26, 60 and 72)* are concerned there is clearly a need to retain a power to return an absconding patient and to have arrangements to deal with cases where the patient absconds shortly before his current period of detention expires. It is proposed in paragraph 2.38, above, that the age limits which now apply to patients suffering from psychopathic disorder or subnormality should be removed; if this is adopted the original reason for providing a six months period for return to hospital of an absconding psychopathic or subnormal patient over 21 will disappear. The main value of the power to enforce return is in relation to the patient who may be a real danger to himself or others, in that it gives power to apprehend him and return him to hospital without requiring a fresh application to be made and so entailing delay. On the other hand, it can be argued that, if a patient has succeeded in remaining out of hospital for as long as 28 days, consideration should be given as to whether the criteria for detention are still met. The simplest way to do this would be by making a fresh application.

8.23 The arguments for retaining a period of only 28 days in relation to section 60 patients are rather less strong. It seems wrong that an offender who has been sent by a court to hospital (in preference to perhaps being committed to prison) because his mental disorder is of a degree which warrants detention in hospital for medical treatment, should, if he succeeds in absconding and remaining at large for 28 days, be able to frustrate the court's intention that he be detained for treatment. MIND point out that the law seems to encourage courts to impose restrictions for fear that a patient might evade the court order and this view also has force. There are however practical difficulties about drawing a distinction between section 26 or section 60 patients in the provision made for returning absconding patients. Staff might be confused as to the powers available for the return of different patients and uncertain as to what information should be passed on to the police and others involved. Moreover, to draw distinctions may well reinforce the reluctance already shown by some staff to deal with offender patients. It is in any case doubtful whether such a distinction need be drawn if the proposal to empower courts to make interim hospital orders is implemented as is suggested in paragraph 5.66, above. If, in the light of previous experience, a court thought that a particular offender might abscond from hospital early it could insure against the risk of losing control over him by initially making an interim hospital order instead of a substantive one. If the patient absconded within the period (up to six months) of such an order he could be arrested without warrant and brought back to the court. The court could then consider imposing a prison sentence.

---

* This would include people detained as if under section 60, eg section 72 patients.

8.24 The Government has therefore concluded that, on balance, the arguments for retaining the same power of compulsory return over absconding section 26 or section 60 patients outweigh those for differentiating between them. It appreciates the fear that the continuation of the present 28 day power might lead to the imposition of restriction orders in cases which do not justify this; but it considers that the making of unnecessary orders is best avoided by revising the wording of section 65 to make it clear that the essential purpose of a restriction order is to protect the public from serious harm, as suggested in paragraph 5.15 above.

### Compulsory Removal of Non-Patrial Psychiatric Patients

8.25 Section 90 empowers the Home Secretary to authorise the compulsory removal from the United Kingdom (and the Isle of Man and the Channel Islands) of a non-patrial patient (that is, one who does not have a right of abode in the United Kingdom) who is receiving treatment for mental illness as a hospital in-patient. The Home Secretary may exercise this power if it appears to him that proper arrangements have been made for the removal and for the care and treatment of the patient in the country to which he is being sent. Directions may be made, as the Home Secretary thinks fit, for the patient's conveyance to the receiving country, including where necessary under escort.

8.26 The main purpose of section 90 is to enable patients who are either irrationally opposed to their removal, or are unable to express a view, to be compulsorily removed to another country when this is judged to be in their best interests. It is also used to enable patients to be kept under escort on their journey home if this is necessary even when the patient has consented to go. Use of section 90 for either purpose is limited in scale—on average about 7 patients per year.

8.27 Section 90 was not discussed in the Consultative Document; since then, the Community Relations Commission (now the Commission for Racial Equality) have suggested—

    i. that section 90 should apply only to patients detained under sections 26 or 60 (ie long term powers);

    ii. that there should be an automatic review by a Mental Health Review Tribunal when use of section 90 is proposed.

They have made other suggestions—on the channelling of enquiries through the International Social Service of Great Britain to ensure that the patient would have a proper standard of care in the receiving country, on the review of procedure and the need to issue guidance—which do not involve legislation and which are being considered separately.

*Should section 90 apply only to patients detained under sections 26 or 60?*

8.28 The status of a patient as 'informal' or 'detained' does not necessarily reflect the degree of his illness, and an informal patient may not necessarily be more able to make rational decisions than a detained patient. The Government accepts it is incongruous that there should be power to remove compulsorily to another country a person who is mentally ill but who is legally entitled to leave hospital at any time. Nor does it seem appropriate that persons subject to short term compulsory orders should be liable to compulsory removal. The Government therefore proposes to adopt the CRE's suggestion and to seek to limit section 90 powers to non-patrial patients detained under sections 26 or 60* of the Act.

*Review of section 90*

8.29 At present there is no right of appeal against a recommendation by a doctor that the Home Secretary uses his powers under section 90. The Government feels that this gap in the review machinery of the Act should not remain and accepts the suggestion made by CRE that Mental Health Review Tribunals would seem the most appropriate agencies for reviewing such recommendations. Such a review would provide a valuable opportunity for the patient to put any reasons he might have for contesting the recommendation. A good deal of thought will need to be given, in consultation with Tribunal Chairmen, to how such a review might best be undertaken. The Government's preliminary view is that it should take place before the case is submitted to the Home Secretary and that the Tribunal should have a power of veto over recommendations for use of section 90, rather than playing an advisory role. Clearly, this would involve Tribunals in work which would be different from that which they carry out at present, insofar as they had to form an opinion on the adequacy of information as to facilities in the receiving country. It would, of course, remain the Home Secretary's responsibility to assure himself that proper arrangements had been made for the removal and the care and treatment of the patient in the country to which he is being sent. The Government therefore proposes that procedures for the automatic review of the use of section 90 should be introduced: the way in which Mental Health Review Tribunals might undertake reviews will be explored with Tribunal Chairmen.

*Powers of recall*

8.30 There is at present no power to recall to hospital a restricted patient who, having been compulsorily removed under section 90, returns to this country. This has occasionally caused difficulty. The Government proposes that the Act should be amended accordingly.

SUMMARY OF PROPOSALS: CHAPTER 8

*Patients' Mail*

i. Section 134, which enables correspondence to and from informal patients to be withheld, should be repealed (para 8.8).

ii. Section 36, which enables correspondence to and from detained patients to be withheld should, with the exception of subsection (2)(a), be repealed (para 8.11).

iii. The power in section 36(2)(a) should be retained. This power enables hospital managers to intercept and withhold correspondence addressed by a detained patient to a person who has given notice in writing that he does not wish to receive such correspondence from the patient concerned (para 8.11).

---

* This would include people detained as if under section 60, eg section 72 patients.

iv.   New powers should be created in respect of patients in Special Hospitals and regional psychiatric secure units.

    a.   Hospital managers should have power to arrange for inspection of correspondence and parcels for the purposes of security and to withhold the contents of a letter or parcel where this is in the interests of the safety of the patient or for the protection of others (paras 8.13 and 8.17);

    b.   The patient should be informed within 24 hours when his mail is inspected or the contents of a letter or parcel are withheld and should have a right of appeal to the hospital managers within 14 days (para 8.14);

    c.   Correspondence between patients in Special Hospitals and regional secure psychiatric units and any one of a specific list of individuals and organisations should not be inspected or withheld except when essential to ensure that in-coming mail comes from the purported source (para 8.15).

### Return of Absconding Patients

v.   Section 40(3), which applies to the period during which an absconding patient may be compulsorily returned to hospital, should no longer apply to short term powers of detention (sections 29, 25 and 30) (para 8.21).

vi.   Section 40 should be amended to provide a period of 28 days for the compulsory return of section 26 or section 60 patients, whatever category of mental disorder they are suffering from (paras 8.22–24).

### Section 90

vii.   Section 90, which allows the compulsory removal from this country of mentally ill hospital in-patients, should be limited to non-patrial patients detained under sections 26 or 60 of the Act (para 8.28).

viii.   Procedures for the automatic review of the use of section 90 should be introduced; the way in which Mental Health Review Tribunals might undertake these reviews will be explored (para 8.29).

ix.   The Act should be amended to provide a power of recall over restricted patients who are compulsorily removed under section 90 and who subsequently return to this country (para 8.30).

CHAPTER 9

# RESOURCE IMPLICATIONS

9.1    This White Paper addresses itself for the most part to changes of emphasis in the compulsory powers provided by the Mental Health Act and to seeking to achieve an improvement in the safeguards provided for patients by means of amendment to the legislation and its associated regulations and forms, and by procedural changes of practice. It is not easy to assess what implications the changes suggested will have for the authorities in terms of manpower or financial resources since most changes will in themselves have only very marginal effects on the workload of the staff concerned; other proposals could have greater significance for the workload of particular individuals. This Chapter sets out the main areas in which there are resource implications, the extent of those implications where an estimate is possible, and the effect on the timing of implementation. As indicated below, it will only be possible to put into effect the proposals with significant resource implications, such as remands to hospital, as and when resources become available.

**Mental Health Review Tribunals**

9.2    In the course of this Paper several proposals have been made which would result in patients having the right to apply more frequently to a Mental Health Review Tribunal and also to have entitlement to automatic review by a Tribunal. It has further been suggested that the powers of Tribunals might be broadened so that they may order delayed discharge and make recommendations on, for example, trial leave. The workload on Tribunals would be increased as a result of such changes, and the Government's estimate is that there would be an increase in fees and expenses of the order of £100,000 per year and of some £50,000 per year in staff costs. These would be met centrally and can be contained within existing expenditure. These proposals also carry unquantifiable implications in respect of extra demands on hospital staff in preparing reports, and on the valuable time of doctors, lawyers and lay members who sit on Tribunals; and, if more use is made of a fourth member, there will be increased demand for local authority social worker time also. However, these proposals are considered sufficiently important to justify implementation as soon as possible following legislation. (See paras 6.1 to 6.13.)

**Age Limits and Treatability**

9.3    The proposed removal of the age limits which at present apply under sections 26 or 33 to psychopathic or subnormal patients would make more people liable to compulsory powers. The strengthening of the treatability criterion would however tend to offset the effect, so it is not thought that there would be a significant change in the number of patients concerned. This proposal is therefore envisaged as one which would become effective shortly after legislation. (See paras 2.38 to 2.40 and 2.45.)

## Health Authorities and Social Services Authorities as Managers

9.4   One of the themes behind several of the changes has been an increasing emphasis on the role of health authorities and social services departments as managers. It is intended that authorities' present functions, such as checking forms, monitoring the use of powers, exercising the right to discharge, will be undertaken more vigorously than has sometimes been the case hitherto. Some authorities do, of course, already carry out their functions very thoroughly so the resource implications for them will not be as great as for others. Although therefore some extra work is likely for both members and staff of some authorities it is felt that in overall terms the resource implications should not be great and should be capable of being met within the steady expansion envisaged in the resources which authorities devote, as suggested in Departmental planning guidelines, to mental health services. (See paras 3.18 to 3.22)

## Remands to Hospital and Interim Hospital Orders

9.5   If courts were given powers to remand mentally disordered defendants to hospital it seems reasonably likely that they would be used in between 1000 and 1500 cases a year although the numbers may eventually prove rather higher. In many, if not most, of the cases, the court would probably wish the defendant to be accommodated in a hospital or unit providing some degree of security thus involving revenue costs higher than those for patients in ordinary psychiatric hospitals. It is estimated that the cost of the provision would be between £1m and £3m (at present prices), depending on the average length of stay, the numbers involved and the extent to which the courts felt able to remand defendants to ordinary psychiatric hospitals and units. The upper figure assumes that all cases will go to secure units. It is not expected that the introduction of interim hospital orders will lead to a much greater demand for hospital places, the best estimate that can be made is that it will require 50 extra hospital places per year at an annual cost of about £250,000. It is proposed that, in the light of these estimates, provision for interim hospital orders might be introduced at an early date after legislation, but for remands to hospital the relevant provision in the new Act would not be brought into operation until the requisite manpower, financial and physical resources were available. (See paras 5.59 to 5.67)

## Automatic Tribunal Reviews for Restricted Patients

9.6   Particular problems exist with this proposal in that many restricted patients are accommodated in the Special Hospitals. The Tribunals in these areas will therefore be faced with a backlog initially and an increased workload. Additional work would also fall upon Home Office staff and on Special Hospital consultants who deal with these references. It is therefore envisaged that, following legislation, a delayed starting date will be set for the implementation of this provision and interim arrangements made in respect of the backlog. (See para 6.4)

## Multi-Disciplinary Panels to Give Second Opinions

9.7   Paragraphs 6.28 and 6.29 of this Paper discuss the need in some cases for a second opinion on treatment to be provided. It is concluded that such provision is necessary and that the second opinion should be given by a multi-disciplinary panel in each Area Health Authority. The composition of the panel has not yet been defined, nor can the number of cases which might be referred be estimated. While the latter might be small, the machinery to apply this safeguard would, nevertheless, be needed. At best, therefore, there would be some additional demands on the time of professional staff involved and some additional work for their support services, in the main the staff of health and local authorities. The establishment of the panels is envisaged as soon as possible following legislation.

### Patients' Advisers

9.8   It is proposed to set up a small number of experimental schemes of patients' advisers as soon as possible to test their functions and effectiveness. These would cost about £50,000 in each of two years and, if it were decided that these schemes should be evaluated independently, then the cost of such evaluation could amount to £10,000 to £15,000 over the two year period. If the experiment proves successful, it is envisaged that adviser schemes would be introduced over the country as part of the planned improvement in mental health services within the resources available. It is estimated that, should schemes be introduced generally on a scale of one per Area Health Authority, the total cost would ultimately build up to about £750,000 per year. (See para 6.35.)

### Safeguards for Staff

9.9   If criminal proceedings were removed from the scope of section 141, there might be some small resource implications for the Office of the Director of Public Prosecutions. This would, however, need to be balanced against some public savings which would result from not having a hearing by a High Court Judge. This provision would come into effect as soon as possible following legislation. (See para 7.5.)

### Compulsory Powers in the Community

9.10   If the proposals on guardianship or alternatives to guardianship were to lead to greater use of powers in the community, there would be additional resource implications for local authorities and different implications for health authorities depending upon the extent to which community care provisions might involve the use of day hospitals and out-patient facilities. The potential demand cannot be estimated, but the powers would be permissive and, as such, would be expected to be used only as local authorities' resources permit. It is envisaged, therefore, that development would be gradual and that the possibilities would be taken into account in the Departmental planning guidance to authorities. (See Chapter 4, especially paras 4.14 to 4.20.)

# APPENDIX
# STATISTICAL DATA

1. This Appendix sets out what statistical information is available from central records on the use of the powers of the Mental Health Act. However, care should be taken in interpreting these as they provide only a general indication of the level of use. This is because statistics are available only in relation to the use of powers at the time of admission to hospital or at discharge from it, and on the status of residents in hospital on a particular day (now 31 December). Information is thus not available about changes of legal status which occur after admission but before discharge. It is not possible to say for example how many patients admitted compulsorily in an emergency (under section 29) become formally detained under longer term powers, or become informal patients, or are discharged. This is also clearly an important limitation from the point of view of describing the extent and duration of the use of, for example, section 26 which will more generally be invoked after admission has been effected under another power.

2. The sources of statistical data used are the Mental Health Enquiry (MHE), statistics obtained by DHSS from health and local authorities, and Criminal Statistics provided by the Home Office. MHE and DHSS statistics record transfers between hospitals and recalls after temporary discharge as well as other admissions. The Home Office Criminal Statistics however do not include transfers or recalls and are therefore not strictly comparable: this Appendix includes statistics on the use of Part V powers from each of the two sources.

TABLE 1.1: *Admission by legal status. 1966, 1970-76 Mental Illness and Mental Handicap Hospitals and Units in England and Wales.*

| Year | Section of the Mental Health Act, 1959 | | | | | | | | | | |
|---|---|---|---|---|---|---|---|---|---|---|---|
| | 25 | 26 | 29 | 30 | 60 (+65) | 72 | 73 | 135 | 136 | Other compulsory powers[3] | Total |
| 1966 | 11,912 | 1,938 | 17,916 | 45 | 1,517 | 159 | 17 | 13 | 1,159 | 447 | 35,123 |
| 1970 | 11,143 | 1,214 | 17,260 | 79 | 1,472 | 117 | 14 | 11 | 1,485 | 350 | 33,145 |
| 1971 | 9,546 | 1,038 | 16,670 | 94 | 1,353 | 106 | 10 | 8 | 1,391 | 268 | 30,484 |
| 1972 | 8,824 | 962 | 15,809 | 126 | 1,219 | 80 | 20 | 8 | 1,495 | 298 | 28,841 |
| 1973 | 8,189 | 861 | 14,916 | 153 | 1,295 | 70 | 16 | 6 | 1,555 | 270 | 27,331 |
| 1974 | 7,452 | 800 | 13,559 | 179 | 1,237 | 60 | 10 | 4 | 1,561 | 219 | 25,081 |
| 1975 | 7,196 | 780 | 12,835 | 206 | 1,278 | 47 | 13 | 9 | 1,600 | 217 | 24,181 |
| 1976 | 6,868 | 791 | 12,057 | 218 | 1,177 | 46 | 11 | 13 | 1,588 | 188 | 22,957 |

[1] *Source*: Mental Health Enquiry.
[2] Figures include Special Hospitals.
[3] For instance, an admission may be recorded under section 47 of the National Assistance Act, 1948.

TABLE 1.2: *Admissions to Mental Illness Hospitals and Units in England and Wales 1966, 1970-76. Informal and Compulsory Admissions.*

| | NUMBERS | | | PROPORTION | |
| YEAR | TOTAL | INFORMAL | COMPULSORY | INFORMAL | COMPULSORY |
|---|---|---|---|---|---|
| 1966 | 170,281 | 136,466 | 33,815 | 80·1% | 19·9% |
| 1970 | 183,510 | 151,447 | 32,063 | 82·5% | 17·5% |
| 1971 | 183,644 | 154,055 | 29,589 | 83·9% | 16·1% |
| 1972 | 185,272 | 157,306 | 27,966 | 84·9% | 15·1% |
| 1973 | 184,726 | 158,200 | 26,526 | 85·6% | 14·4% |
| 1974 | 181,451 | 157,015 | 24,436 | 86·5% | 13·5% |
| 1975 | 186,215 | 162,714 | 23,501 | 87·4% | 12·6% |
| 1976 | 190,358 | 168,084 | 22,274 | 88·3% | 11·7% |

[1] *Source*: Mental Health Enquiry.
[2] Figures include Special Hospitals.

TABLE 1.3: *Admissions to Mental Handicap Hospitals and Units in England and Wales 1966, 1970-76. Informal and Compulsory Admissions.*

| | NUMBERS | | | PROPORTION | |
| YEAR | TOTAL | INFORMAL | COMPULSORY | INFORMAL | COMPULSORY |
|---|---|---|---|---|---|
| 1966 | 10,887 | 9,579 | 1,308 | 88% | 12% |
| 1970 | 11,593 | 10,511 | 1,082 | 90·7% | 9·3% |
| 1971 | 12,155 | 11,260 | 895 | 92·6% | 7·4% |
| 1972 | 12,624 | 11,749 | 875 | 93·1% | 6·9% |
| 1973 | 12,462 | 11,657 | 805 | 93·5% | 6·5% |
| 1974 | 12,937 | 12,292 | 645 | 95% | 5% |
| 1975 | 13,914 | 13,234 | 680 | 95·1% | 4·9% |
| 1976 | 15,262 | 14,579 | 683 | 95·5% | 4·5% |

[1] *Source*: Mental Health Enquiry.
[2] Figures include Special Hospitals.

TABLE 1.4: *Admissions of offenders under Part V. 1966, 1970-76 Mental Illness and Mental Handicap Hospitals and Units in England and Wales.*

| Year | Section of the Mental Health Act | | | | | |
|------|-----------|----------------------------------|-----------|-------------------------------|-------------------------------|-------|
| | Section 60 | Section 60 with Section 65 | Section 72 | Section 72 with Section 74 | Section 73 with Section 74 | TOTAL |
| 1966 | 1,259 | 181 | 16 | 133 | 16 | 1,605 |
| 1970 | 1,039 | 278 | 18 | 89 | 17 | 1,441 |
| 1971 | 954 | 232 | 7 | 89 | 16 | 1,298 |
| 1972 | 832 | 214 | 15 | 62 | 29 | 1,152 |
| 1973 | 888 | 266 | 4 | 56 | 19 | 1,233 |
| 1974 | 808 | 196 | 4 | 40 | 12 | 1,060 |
| 1975 | 861 | 156 | 5 | 39 | 15 | 1,076 |
| 1976 | 773 | 151 | 6 | 37 | 13 | 980 |

[1] *Source*: Home Office Criminal Statistics for England and Wales.
[2] Figures include Special Hospitals.


TABLE 2.1: *Residents by legal status at 31 December. 1974-6[1] Mental Illness and Mental Handicap Hospitals and Units in England and Wales.*

| YEAR | SECTION OF MENTAL HEALTH ACT. | | | | | | | Other compulsory Powers | TOTAL |
|------|------|-------|-----|----|---------|-------|---------|---------|-------|
| | 25 | 26 | 29 | 30 | 60(+65) | 72+73 | 135+136 | | |
| 1974 | 1,107 | 2,834 | 128 | 20 | 2,734 | 251 | 23 | 796 | 7,893 |
| 1975 | 1,272 | 2,717 | 102 | 16 | 2,673 | 257 | 4 | 639 | 7,680 |
| 1976 | 985 | 2,725 | 101 | 22 | 2,595 | 251 | 9 | 580 | 7,268 |

[1] Figures for previous years are not comparable as the method of collection was revised for 1974.
[2] *Source*: Form SHB 13C.
[3] Figures include Special Hospitals.

TABLE 2.2: *Residents in Mental Illness and Mental Handicap Hospitals and Units in England and Wales. 1974-76[1]. Informal and Compulsory Residents[2].*

| | | NUMBERS | | PROPORTION | |
|---|---|---|---|---|---|
| YEAR | TOTAL | INFORMAL | COMPULSORY | INFORMAL | COMPULSORY |
| 1974 | 150,857 | 142,964 | 7,893 | 94·8% | 5·2% |
| 1975 | 146,718 | 139,038 | 7,680 | 94·8% | 5·2% |
| 1976 | 142,272 | 135,004 | 7,268 | 94·9% | 5∶1% |

[1] Figures for previous years are not comparable as the method of collection was revised for 1974.
[2] *Source*: SBH 13C.
[3] Figures include Special Hospitals.


TABLE 3: *Use of Guardianship powers under sections 33 and 60 for Mentally Ill and Mentally Handicapped People in England and Wales; 1966, 1970-76.*

| Date | Mentally Ill | Mentally Handicapped | Total[2] |
|---|---|---|---|
| 21 December 1966 | 17 | 302 | 319 (9) |
| 31 December 1970 | 22 | 207 | 229 (5) |
| 31 March 1972[3] | | | 223 (4) |
| 31 March 1973 | 24 | 165 | 189 (8) |
| 31 March 1974 | 25 | 134 | 159 (7) |
| 31 March 1975 | 27 | 141 | 168 (4) |
| 31 March 1976 | 24 | 118 | 142 (4) |

[1] *Source:* SSDA 702 and Home Office Criminal Statistics.
[2] Figures in parentheses are the numbers of guardianship orders under section 60 in each year.
[3] No data is available for 1971; nor is there any analysis of the total figure for 1972 (for England) as between Mentally Ill and Mentally Handicapped persons; the figures for Wales were – 1 mentally ill person and 4 mentally handicapped persons.

# GLOSSARY OF TERMS

*Aarvold Committee*

Committee set up under the chairmanship of Sir Carl Aarvold, OBE, TD, in June 1972 to advise whether any changes, within the existing law, were required in the procedures for the discharge and supervision of patients subject to special restrictions under section 65 of the Mental Health Act 1959. The Committee reported in January 1973 (Cmnd 5191).

*Advisory Board*

Board set up following the Aarvold Committee's report to advise the Home Secretary on the discharge and supervision of psychiatric patients subject to special restrictions.

*Age limits*

Patients suffering from psychopathic disorder and subnormality may not be compulsorily admitted to hospital under section 26 of the Act or received into guardianship under section 33, if aged 21 or over. If compulsorily admitted before the age of 21, they may be detained until they are 25 but cannot be detained after that unless they are likely to be dangerous if discharged.

*'Approved' doctor*

A doctor who has special experience in the diagnosis or treatment of mental disorder and is approved by the Area Health Authority under section 28 of the Mental Health Act for the purpose of making medical recommendations.

*Butler Committee*

Committee established in September 1972 under the chairmanship of the Rt Hon the Lord Butler of Saffron Walden, KG, CH, to consider the position of mentally abnormal offenders before the law, and the means of dealing with such offenders. Reported in 1975 (Cmnd 6244). An interim Report was published in 1974 (Cmnd 5698).

*Compulsory admission*

Admission for observation or treatment made without the person's consent on the basis of an application by a relative, usually the nearest relative, or a Mental Welfare Officer, supported by one or two medical recommendations.

*Consultative Document*

'A Review of the Mental Health Act 1959' published in August 1976 inviting comments on how the Act might be amended.

*Crisis intervention service*

A 24 hour emergency service in the community provided by a multi-professional therapeutic team to deal with psychiatric crises.

### Detained (formal) patient

A patient who is subject to one of the compulsory powers in the Act and who may be compelled to remain in hospital.

### (Under) Disability in relation to the trial

Phrase proposed by the Butler Committee to replace the present term 'unfit to plead' (Cmnd 6244, para 10.2).

### Guardianship

The compulsory placement of a person into the care and control of a local authority or a person approved by the local social services authority as guardian. The guardian has the same powers as a father has over a child of under 14 years. (See sections 33 and 60, under '*Long term Powers*').

### Hospital managers

Authorities which have duties under the Act in relation to the compulsory admission, renewal of detention and discharge of detained patients. Area Health Authorities act as managers of local psychiatric hospitals and the Department of Health and Social Security manages the Special Hospitals.

### Informal (voluntary) patient

A patient who has entered hospital or remains in hospital without compulsion.

### Long term powers

Section 26—Detention for treatment which lasts initially for 1 year and is renewable for a further period of 1 year and then for 2 years at a time. Applications may be made by the nearest relative or a Mental Welfare Officer and must be supported by 2 medical recommendations.

Section 60—Admission to hospital for treatment on the order of a court, made in criminal proceedings, on the basis of 2 medical recommendations. The order lasts for the same period as powers under section 26, unless a restriction order under section 65 is also made. Alternatively, a court may place the person concerned into guardianship.

Section 65—Imposition of special restrictions upon offenders already subject to a section 60 order. (See '*Restriction Order*').

Section 33—Enables a person to be placed under guardianship on the application of the nearest relative or a Mental Welfare Officer and with 2 medical recommendations. The powers last for the same periods as those under section 26. (See '*Guardianship*').

### Medical recommendation

Formal written recommendation made by a doctor in support of an application for compulsory admission or renewal of detention.

### Medical treatment

See paragraph 1.23.

*Mental Health Review Tribunal*
Tribunal which, following application by the patient or his nearest relative or on request by the Home Secretary, reviews the necessity for detention of patients; Tribunals, in the case of 'unrestricted' patients, have the right to order discharge, and they advise the Home Secretary on the need for discharge of 'restricted' patients.

*Mental Welfare Commission*
Established in Scotland under the Mental Health (Scotland) Act, 1960 and consisting of at least 7 and not more than 11 commissioners of whom one is chairman, at least one a woman, at least 3 medical practitioners and one a lawyer. The primary duty of the Commission is 'generally to exercise protective functions in respect of persons who may, by reason of mental disorder, be incapable of adequately protecting their persons or their interests'.

*Mental Welfare Officer*
Officer appointed by the local social services authority to make applications for compulsory admission and carry out certain other functions in connection with the Act.

*Nearest relative*
Relative who comes first in the hierarchy set out in section 49 of the Act and who has certain powers in relation to applications for compulsory admission and certain rights to order discharge of a detained patient.

*Part IV*
That part of the Act which relates to compulsory powers over non-offender patients.

*Part V*
That part of the Act which relates to patients involved in criminal proceedings and the transfer to hospital of mentally disordered prisoners.

*Place of Safety*
A place in which a person suspected of being mentally disordered can be detained, for the purpose of a medical examination and with a view to the making of any necessary arrangements for his treatment or care. The power of detention (see sections 135 and 136) lasts for up to 72 hours. (See para 2.24)

*Powers in relation to offender patients*
Section 60—see '*Long term Powers*'.

Section 72—Enables the Home Secretary to direct the transfer to hospital of a sentenced prisoner who is suffering from mental illness, psychiatric disorder, subnormality or severe subnormality, to a degree which warrants his detention in hospital for medical treatment.

Section 73—Enables the Home Secretary to authorise the removal to hospital of unsentenced prisoners suffering from mental illness or severe subnormality whose condition warrants detention in hospital for medical treatment.

### Regional secure psychiatric units
Units being set up in each health service region in England for mentally disordered patients who require more security than can be provided by local hospitals but not of the degree provided by the Special Hospitals.

### Responsible Medical Officer
Doctor responsible for the treatment of a detained patient. He has certain statutory functions, for example in relation to the renewal of detention, discharge, the granting of trial leave and the withholding of his patients' mail.

### Restriction order
Order which may be imposed by the court under section 65 of the Act in addition to a section 60 hospital order. It has the effect of requiring the Home Secretary's consent to leave of absence, transfer to another hospital and discharge.

### Restricted patient
Offender patient subject to a restriction order under section 65.

### Royal Commission 1954/57
The Royal Commission on the Law Relating to Mental Illness and Mental Deficiency. Report published May 1957. (The Percy Commission) Cmnd 169.

*Sections* 29, 25, 30, 135, 136—see *Short term powers.*

*Sections* 26, 60, 33—see *Long term powers.*

*Sections* 72, 73—see *Powers in relation to offender patients.*

### Short-term powers
Section 29—Emergency admission for observation on the basis of an application from any relative or a Mental Welfare Officer and of a recommendation by a doctor.

Section 25—Admission for up to 28 days for observation (with or without other medical treatment) on the basis of an application from the nearest relative of a Mental Welfare Office and of recommendations by 2 doctors.

Section 135—Empowers a justice to authorise a police constable to enter private premises and to remove from there to a 'place of safety' (see above) a person believed to be mentally disordered or who is absent without leave from hospital.

Section 136—Empowers a police constable to remove an apparently mentally disordered person from a public place to a 'place of safety' (see above).

Section 30—Provides for the detention for up to 3 days of an informal patient who is already in hospital on the basis of a report from the doctor in charge of the patient's treatment.

## Special Hospitals
Hospitals provided for detained patients who, in the opinion of the Secretary of State, require treatment under conditions of special security because of their dangerous, violent or criminal propensities.

## 'Treatability'
The likelihood that there will be benefit from treatment.

## Unrestricted patients
Patients who are not subject to a section 65 restriction order.

Printed in England for Her Majesty's Stationery Office by Bemrose Specialist Print Ltd.
Dd. 294786 K120 9/78